MW00462045

FOR OTHER BOOKS & RESOURCES
BY JACOB REEVE, GO TO:

www.thegoldenlampstand.com

The Great
Procession

Jacob Reeve

The Great Procession
Copyright © 2013 Jacob Reeve

All rights reserved. Written permission must be secured from the author to use or reproduce any part of this book, except for brief and critical reviews or articles.

The Great Procession website: www.thegreatprocession.com

Unless otherwise indicated, all scripture quotations are taken from the New American Standard Bible, Copyright © 1960, 1962, 1963, 1968, 1971, 1972, 1973, 1975, 1977 by The Lockman Foundation.

Printed in the United States of America.

To my wife Kimberly, and to all my children, for your love and support for me and for the sacrifices you made to allow me to complete this book. My love is forever yours.

To my friends and editors, Robyn Custer, Alex Padua, Melissa Perez, Israel Ramirez, Hieu Nguyen & Christine Fry. The gift of your time and talents and your service to Christ is deeply appreciated. Thank you.

Most of all, to the Holy Spirit, for being my dearest instructor and source of inspiration. I love You. You are truly beautiful. Thank you for Your eternal sacrifice and service to us all.

CONTENTS

PREFACE

This book is my attempt to put into words the most extraordinary and amazing time of my life. Plain and simple, I met the Holy Spirit, and over a nine month period, He visited me almost every night in order to tell me an ongoing story, each night picking up where He left off the night before. My hope is that the Spirit of God will use this book to catch you up into the ecstasies of His infinite grace and council.

I Corinthians 14:32 says, "the spirits of the prophets are subject to the prophets."

Because prophecy is subjective by nature, all prophecies, including the observations I make in this book, should not be held as absolute unless the scriptures reveal them as such. There are some who do not believe in the prophetic gift and others who have given up on it because of a bad experiences. To those, Paul says, "Do not grieve the Holy Spirit, do not despise prophetic utterances. Examine everything carefully and hold fast to that which is good." - 1 Thessalonians 5:19-21

This is exactly what I am asking you to do as a reader. I do believe that God wants us to consider this account carefully and to take those conclusions seriously. The things the Lord revealed to me in these pages have had a deep and profound impact on the way I live and relate to Him, myself and others. I believe the revelation in this book is extremely relevant and offers many answers for both individuals as well as the body of Christ at large.

1 Corinthians 14 says that if someone prophesies, others should pass judgment on the prophecy. Please make judgments on the things written in this book. The gifts of the Holy Spirit are for the glorification of Christ

(John 16:13-14) and for the edification of the saints (1 Cor. 14:12). If anything does not ultimately bring glory to Christ or is not edifying, please feel free to discard it.

I offer these prior statements out of my concern that in releasing this book, people would think I am insisting that all of the things revealed here are set in stone and that I hold them as absolutes. This is not true. While I do believe that the words in this book do reveal truth, I affirm the scriptures as the final authority on the doctrine and testimony of the New Covenant. True revelation should never contradict any foundational scriptural doctrine, and most of all, true doctrine should not contradict Christ. In writing this vision, I have merely tried to be faithful in communicating the series of pictures that I have seen in a way that is easy for others to comprehend. I have tested these things and decided they are good. Now it is up to the reader to test them and discern what is correct and what is applicable.

I also want to confess a fear that people might think of me as being more spiritual than others because I have seen this vision. I do not hold this opinion of myself. I believe the Holy Spirit is present for all to learn from and talk to as their closest friend and guide (John 14:26; 16:12-14). I must insist here that it should not be uncommon that we hear the Holy Spirit in a definitive way. I believe hearing the Spirit is so important to God and so under experienced by the church that I have included a short scripture study on the following pages to explain this essential new covenant reality.

SCRIPTURE STUDY ON THE GUIDANCE OF THE HOLY SPIRIT

The Holy Spirit is the Teacher and Guide of the New Covenant.

There is so much that God has given us in Christ. The Holy Spirit being the greatest of all His glorious gifts! With the Holy Spirit comes abundant and everlasting access to the thoughts and feelings of God. One of the greatest blessings of being immersed in the Holy Ghost is the access we have to the word of God. That is, communication, strait from God to us through His Spirit!

Hundreds of years before the incarnation of Christ, Jeremiah 31:33-34 prophesies of the day when God's Spirit would be poured out upon all flesh and that we would each be able to commune with God as individuals, without any earthly priest or teacher between us and Him.

Jeremiah 31:33-34 says, "But this shall be the covenant that I will make..." said the LORD. "I will put my law in their inward parts, and write it in their hearts; and will be their God, and they shall be my people. And they shall teach no more every man his neighbor, and every man his brother, saying, 'Know the LORD:' for they shall all know me, from the least of them unto the greatest of them," said the LORD. "For I will forgive their iniquity, and I will remember their sin no more."

The New Testament makes it clear that this prophecy was fulfilled on the day of Pentecost, 50 days after Christ was crucified. We should all know the Lord plainly now through His Spirit.

In John chapter 14, Jesus gives His commentary on the coming age of our union with Him through His Spirit. "I will ask the Father to give you another Helper, to be with you always. He is the Spirit of truth, whom the world cannot receive, for it neither sees Him nor recognizes Him. But you recognize Him, for He abides with you and will be in you. I have told you this while I am still with you... But the Helper, the Holy Spirit, whom the Father will send in my name, will teach you all things and remind you of all that I have told you" (John 14:16-26).

In John chapter 16, Jesus again affirms the age of the Holy Spirit, when everyone will be able to hear His voice plainly. He says, "However, I am telling you the truth. It is for your advantage that I am going away, for if I do not go away the Helper will not come to you. But if I go, I will send Him to you. When He comes, He will convict the world of sin, righteousness, and judgment... Yet when the Spirit of Truth comes, He will guide you into all truth. For He will not speak on His own accord, but will speak whatever He hears and will declare to you the things that are to come. He will glorify me, for He will take what is mine and declare it to you" (John 16:7-14)

In Acts chapter 2, the day of pentecost had come and the Holy Spirit had fallen upon everyone in the upper room. Peter then, being filled with the Spirit, began explaining to all the bystanders that the Holy Spirit was now being released upon all people as a fulfillment of prophecy. Look at the prophecy Peter quotes. "These men are not drunk as you suppose, for it's only nine o'clock in the morning. Rather, this is what was spoken through the prophet Joel. 'In the last days, God says, I will pour out my Spirit on everyone. Your sons and your daughters will prophesy, your young men will see visions, and your old men will dream dreams. In those days I will even pour out my Spirit on my slaves, men and women alike, and they will prophesy.'" (Acts 2:15-18)

In 2 Corinthians chapter 3 Paul describes a few New Covenant realities regarding the Holy Spirit. He says, "You are demonstrating that you are Christ's letter, produced by our service, written not with ink but with the Spirit of the living God, not on tablets of stone but on tablets of human hearts..." (2 Cor. 3:3). "[God] has also qualified us to be ministers of a new covenant, which is not of the letter but of the spirit, for the letter kills, but the Spirit gives life." (2 Cor. 3:6).

1 John 2:27 also confirms that we are all expected to hear God directly through the anointing within each one of us. "The anointing you received from Him abides in you, and you do not need anyone to teach you.

Instead, because His anointing teaches you about everything and is true and not a lie, abide in Him, as He taught you to do" (1 John 2:27).

So, it is clear that under the New Covenant we no longer need anyone but Christ to be a mediator between us and God. He has deposited the Holy Spirit into His people so that we may receive all instruction and revelation directly from Him in a personal and intimate way.

Hebrews 5:12 says, "For though by this time you ought to be teachers, you still have need for someone to teach you the elementary principals of the oracles of God, and you have come to need milk instead of solid food."

The scriptures make it clear that God does sanction teaching, but teaching's main task should always be to bring people to the point where they personally know God and are empowered by Him to feed and teach themselves. Good teaching is a product of good teachers who have wisdom, love and experience in their knowledge of God (Heb. 5:14, 1 Tim. 1:5). The point of teaching is not to know the scriptures, but to know Christ Himself through His Spirit.

In John 5:39, Jesus says, "You search the scriptures because you think that in them you have eternal life, but it is these that testify about Me."

The Holy Spirit is essential to our experience of the Kingdom of God.

As you read the New Testament Gospels, you can scarcely go a chapter without finding Jesus talking about "the Kingdom of God." The Sermon on the Mount began with the "Kingdom" and ended with the "Kingdom" with seven other references to the "Kingdom" in between (Matt. 5-7). The Lord's Prayer begins with, "Your Kingdom come," and ends with, "For Yours is the Kingdom..." (Matt. 6:9-13). The vast majority of Jesus' parables begin by saying, "The Kingdom of God is like..." Jesus said, "I must preach the Gospel of the Kingdom of God... for that is what I came for." (Luke 4:43). The Kingdom of God is undoubtedly the central theme of Christ's earthly teaching. The Kingdom was the thing He came to preach, teach and establish.

During the time of His earthly ministry, Jesus continued to talk about how the Kingdom of God was at hand. He talked about the day that was coming when His Spirit would be released and we would all be able to know Him just as mentioned in the previous scriptures. The Kingdom of God is (the place of) God's dominion. It is the place He and His will are both known and kept. In the New Covenant we experience the power of this Kingdom in direct proportion to the amount that we experience His Holy Spirit. In this dispensation our experience and emersion into the Kingdom of God is the same as our experience and emersion into the Holy Spirit.

During the incarnation of Christ the power of the kingdom of God had not been established on earth yet.   However, it would come in power during the lifetime of the disciples. Mark 9:1 says, "And Jesus was saying to them, 'Truly I say to you, there are some of those who are standing here who will not taste death until they see the Kingdom of God after it has come in power.'"

Jesus said that the power of the Kingdom of God would be established on earth when the Holy Spirit came upon the disciples. Acts 1:6-8 says, "So when they had come together, they were asking Him saying, 'Lord, is it at this time that You are restoring the kingdom...' He said to them... 'You will receive power when the Holy Spirit has come upon you.'" Further, Jesus says in John 3:5, "Truly, truly I say unto you, unless one is born of water and of Spirit, he cannot enter the Kingdom of God." The "coming upon" of the Spirit was inarguably experienced on the day of Pentecost (Acts 2:1-4) and has remained ever since.

In the New Covenant, therefore, we know God's kingdom to the extent that we know the Holy Spirit. This being true, we should all know the Holy Spirit, being able to say that He speaks to us and directs us in a definitive way.

This is exactly the practice we see modeled for us in the book of Acts. It says in Acts, "the Spirit said unto Philip..." (Acts 8:29); "The Spirit said unto Peter..." (Acts 10:19); "And the Spirit told me go with them..." (Acts 11:12); "The Spirit did not allow them..." (Acts 16:7); and "They said to Paul through the Spirit..." (Acts 21:4). Hearing the voice of the Holy Spirit in a definitive way is both normal and common in the New Testament church.

The scriptures also affirm dreams (Mt. 1:20; 2:12-13; Acts 2:17), visions (Luke 1:22; 24:23; Acts 2:17; 9:10-12; 10:3-19; 12:9; 16:9-10; 18:9; 2 Cor. 12:1; Revelation) and prophecy (Acts 2:17-18; 19:6; 21:9; Rom.12:6; 1 Tim.1:18, etc.) as a normative means of communication between God and man in the New Covenant. The New Testament church was able to say with confidence and without question, "The Spirit said to me..." We are still the New Testament church and we should know the Lord to such an extent that we can say the same. 2 Tim.1:7 says, "God has not given us a spirit of timidity, but of power, love, and self discipline."

Having said this, I would add here as a caution, just because we believe the Spirit is speaking something, it doesn't mean that we should automatically receive it as infallible. It should be tested (1 John 4:1), judged (1Cor.14:29), weighed according to the scriptures, and even then, it is still subject to the prophet (1Cor.14:32).

AN INTRODUCTION

In July of 2005, our lease was up and my wife Kimberly and I began praying about where God wanted us to live. When I prayed, I clearly saw a scripture reference pop into my mind. It said, "2 Samuel 7:5-6." I turned to the passage and read:

"Would you build a house for Me to dwell in? For I have not dwelt in a house since the time that I brought the children of Israel up from Egypt, even to this day, but have moved about in a tent and in a tabernacle."

"Wow!" I thought, "This passage is talking about houses!" I read it a second time to see how it might be applied to our situation. Upon reading it over, I thought, "Is God telling me to move into a tent? There is no way I would ask my wife, who is pregnant to move into a tent."

When I got home, Kimberly asked me if I heard anything about where we were supposed to move and I said, "Not really." I asked if she received anything and she said "Yes, when I prayed God showed me the passage, Joshua 18:1. It says:

"Now the whole congregation of the children of Israel assembled together at Shiloh, and set up the tabernacle of meeting there. And the land was subdued before them."

She said, "I think we are supposed to move into a tent at Shiloh." Located in the heart of a densely populated college party town, Shiloh was a ministry house that we had started where 20 other people lived. To me it was the equivalent of God saying, "Move into a tent in downtown San Francisco or Compton or Sodom & Gomorrah."

I was shocked! I said, "God gave me a scripture about moving into a tent too, but there is no way I am going to let you and our three kids move into a tent at Shiloh. God would have to confirm that a lot more before I would put you all in harms way like that."

We told no one, but over the course of the next three weeks, 9 different people came up to us at different times either with dreams or scriptures that had to do with us giving up all our possessions and moving into tents. One of them actually handed Kimberly a tiny ripped piece of paper with Joshua 18:1 written on it, the exact same passage that Kimberly had received.

We were trapped. We could not deny that God was calling my pregnant wife Kimberly and me to give up the majority of our possessions and live in a tent with our three children, ages 4, 3, and 1. So we did.

At first I had some hope that some amazing or miraculous thing would happen as a result, but the longer time went on, the harder it was to perceive any reason why God would have wanted us to live there. I felt embarrassed I was not providing better for my wife so I kept trying to move us into different places. But every time we stepped into a potential house to rent, the word "treason" immediately came to both of us. We both became extremely uncomfortable just standing in these potential rentals. We were stuck. I was willing to do almost anything to get us into a house, but my wife kept insisting that God had called us to live in a tent. Therefore we needed to stay in a tent until He called us back out. She is an amazing, faithful woman of God. Yet even with her confidence, we were struggling. We were not struggling as much in our marriage, nor were we struggling with the question of if we had heard God correctly. We were wondering *why* God wanted us in a tent. We were also struggling with issues of comfort and functionality. Being a pastor, it seemed like this move had made me far less productive and useful to the church than I had been previously.

One day in particular I was very depressed. It was not just the tent, but a multitude of things. On this day I was scheduled to speak at a Bible college about four hours south. As I was leaving, deep despair came over me and I began to cry. I didn't want to be around anyone–which is hard to do if you are living in a tent, on a community house yard, in the middle of a populated city. So I got in my car and began crying out to God. In my outburst, I did something very stupid. I said, "Why don't you just kill me."

As I sobered up and began to drive away, I suddenly became very afraid for my family that God might allow me to die. I began imagining ways that I might die a car accident or a disease or a hold up. I started begging God to spare me on behalf of my wife and kids. Haha! Because of His mercy, God spared me.

The next day at the Bible College, they had taken the day off of classes to have a full day of prayer. During a time of corporate worship I saw a vision of a castle. Within ten minutes, I had received two more castle pictures. At the time I received these three pictures, I didn't think much of them, but because they had come in such a short time, they were all related to each other, and I was in such a spiritually charged environment when I received them, I thought God might be trying to communicate something to me. Therefore I illustrated the three pictures in my note book so I would remember them in case God wanted to later reveal something to me through them.

A few days after I had returned home from the Bible College, God finally released us to move out of the tent and lease a house. As we moved out we heard that the Jewish feast, Sukkot was just ending. Sukkot is the "Feast of Booths," or "Tents." We found that we had been experiencing the same thing the Israelites must have been experiencing in the wilderness when they had to dwell in tents. We also began receiving the revelation about why God likes to dwell in tents more than permanent structures. He is content to dwell in the tabernacle of His people. As you read on in this book, you will see this come up time and again.

Two weeks later on my 30th birthday, I began a 40 day fast. As the Levites would move into the office of a priest when they turned 30, so I too believed God was calling me into a type of priesthood, which would officially begin when I turned 30. This is why I decided to do the fast. I wanted to dedicate the first 40 days of my priesthood (adulthood) to God so I decided to give Him undivided attention for the first 40 days. Two days after my fast began, our fourth child was born. Her name is Goldie.

The fast was miserable. I had so much work to do with our new baby and our three other children (ages four, three and one). I didn't seem to have much time to spend seeking God. However, every time I did get a moment to spare, I would ask God three questions;:"What do You want my priesthood to look like," "What do You want my family to look like," and "What do You want Your church to look like?"

Every day God was silent. For four weeks I could not find God anywhere. I realize now that sometimes His silence puts more emphasis on what He is about to say. About four weeks into fasting and asking, God finally answered. The answer was not directly about me, but He spoke it as a result of my asking and for this reason it meant the world to me. I asked, "Lord, What do You want my life to look like?" There was no answer. I asked, "Lord, what do You want my family to look like?" Again, there was no answer. I then asked, "Lord, what do You want Your church to look like?" Then He spoke loud and clear, "I want My church to look like My Kingdom!"

It was as clear a reply as I have ever heard. It was not audible, but it was a resounding statement within my spirit that I could not get rid of for many weeks. Even to this day, I hear these very words in my head every time I think of the church. At first, I didn't know what this meant. I began to do a Bible study on the subject of the Kingdom of God. For a whole week I saw little parallel between the Church as I knew it and the Kingdom of God as revealed in the scriptures. After a week of studying the kingdom of God and struggling to see the parallels between the Kingdom and the Church, I began questioning if I had even heard the Lord correctly. It seemed like the Kingdom of God and my experience of the church were entirely separate and incompatible. At this time, the Lord spoke again, "That is the problem." These two sentences were all that I received as far as personal instruction the entire time I fasted.

On the third night after the fast had ended I was awoken abruptly at around 2am. I had a vivid picture in my mind of the castle that I had seen a few months earlier when I was at the Bible College. The only difference was this time, I could hear a warm, loving voice narrating the story behind what I was seeing. From that day forward, the Holy Spirit began to visit me almost every night. Around 2am, He would wake me up to a vision and speak to me about it. Most nights He would either pick up where He left off the night before or He would take me back into a picture I had already seen and explain it to me.

The next year, the Lord revealed more clearly to us about why He had called us to live in a tent. During a prayer meeting, my friend Liz started naming all the sacrificial and illogical things God called the prophets to do in the Old Testament. She spoke of how God called Isaiah to prophesy naked for three years and then she asked, "Who are you God?" Then she talked about how God told Hosea to marry a prostitute, and the agony it brought him. Then she asked, "Who are you God?" She then explained how God called Ezekiel to lie on his side and eat food cooked over cow dung for well over a year and then when he was finally finished, God took his wife and commanded him not to mourn for her. Then she asked, "Who are you God?" Then she answered and said something along the line of, "When God receives someone who has willfully surrendered their lives to Him as a prophet and a bond slave, He honors them by not just using their mouths, but their lives to communicate whatever statement He desires."

It hit me hard when she said it. Hebrews 11:8-10 instantly came to mind. I turned there in my bible and read, "By faith Abraham, when he was called, obeyed going out into a place which he should receive later for an inheritance; and he went out, not knowing where he went. By faith he sojourned in the land of promise, as in a strange country, dwelling in tents with Isaac and Jacob, the heirs with him of the same promise: For he was looking for a city which has foundations, whose architect and builder is God." I believe that, in a small way, God wanted the actions of my family to be a prophetic word to our own fellowship, who, only nine months later, happened to lose our large meeting place and decided to move into a big tent. I also believe this is a word for the larger church in general. God is saying that He is looking for a people who are not as comfortable with earthly securities and structures as they are with seeking a kingdom with foundations, whose architect and builder is God. He is saying that He wants to dwell on earth in the tent of our bodies while we dwell in heaven in the tent of His body.

Years later as I look back I realize that the two simple statements I received from God during my fast would sum up the whole meaning of this series of revelations that I have received in this book. God is calling His church to come out from the kingdom of death and darkness and into the Kingdom of life and light in Jesus Christ. If this vision is from Him, then God is saying, "I want My Church to look like My Kingdom." Will you allow Him to shake all that is not built on Him alone!

"But now He has promised, saying, 'Yet once more I will shake not only the earth but the heavens.' This expression, 'Yet once more,' denotes the removing of those things which can be shaken, as of created things, so that

those things which cannot be shaken may remain. Therefore, since we are receiving a Kingdom which cannot be shaken, let us show gratitude, by which we may offer to God an acceptable service with reverence and awe; for our God is a consuming fire." (Hebrews 12:26-29).

...Every scribe who is trained for the kingdom of heaven is like unto a man that is like the master of a household which brings forth out of his treasure things both new and old (Matthew 13:52).

May the God of our Lord Jesus Christ, the Father of glory, give to you a spirit of wisdom and of revelation in the knowledge of Him. *I pray* the eyes of your heart be enlightened, so that you will know the hope of His calling, the riches of the glory of His inheritance in the saints, and the surpassing greatness of His power toward us who believe.

THE BIG PICTURE

In this series of visions, the Holy Spirit takes me on a journey from the kingdom of death and darkness into the kingdom of life and light. The kingdom of death is pictured as a stone castle which represents man's religious law with a river mote that runs around it; representing man's lust. The kingdom of life is represented by a forest on top of a hill. There is a path that leads from the castle of death to the hill and its forest of life. The people on this path face many trials and temptations. Some will fall, others will rise.

Each stone within the castle represents a false religion, belief, ideology, or law into which people, especially church people, place their identity and security. In this vision I see a large number of people within this generation making an exodus out from the stone walls of the castle of religion. At first, as they leave the castle, they do not know exactly where they are going, but every step they take is one that brings more clarity and light to them. In the landscape of truth, ground can only be gained through accepting the revelation of the Truth. It is a journey into their true identity in Christ.

Generally speaking, the world that we are most familiar with is the material world. But there is also an equally, if not more real, spiritual world in which we live. This vision is not at all meant to be a picture of the material world but a picture of the spiritual world. In the material world we can say, I am in such-in-such a place. We understand that there is a present location of our physical bodies. It is the same in the spiritual world. In the spiritual world we are also in a certain specific location. It is my prayer that this vision will help you identify where you are in relation to Him.

Chapter 1

Faith

I WAS STANDING ON THE SIDE of a dirt path about three fourths of the way up a grassy hill. At the top of the hill, behind and to the left of me, the path led into a forest with larger mountains behind it. In front of me the path wound down and slightly to the left. It ended at the bottom of the hill where I saw the front of a castle made of stone. The castle had a mote which appeared to flow all the way around, making the land on which the castle rested a small island. The castle's gate could be lowered into a drawbridge over the mote.

A moment later, the drawbridge lowered and as it did, I saw there was a great multitude of people who were waiting within the gate. Excitement, expectation and anxiety seemed to mark the crowd as they smashed together, pressing tighter and tighter into the opening. But on the right, I noticed there was a man who stood alone. He faced out and was holding what looked like a balloon in his right hand. But as the drawbridge lowered, the balloon took on more and more the form of a banner. The lever which released the drawbridge was being tightly gripped by the left hand of this man. He was the one who released the lever that caused the gate to become a bridge.

For some reason I was drawn to the drawbridge in an unusual way; there was something wonderful about it. I enjoyed the feeling I got from just looking at it.

After some time, my thoughts returned again to the man who held the banner and released the lever in the gate.

The Spirit said, "The name on the banner is joy. Thanksgiving, praise, and worship open these gates and lower these pathways." As He spoke, his words seemed to flow directly into my stomach and spine, without the need to pass through my ears.

He was saying this banner holder represented those who were true worshipers—not necessarily just in music, but in attitude. They were like true Levite musicians—the first on the battle field, the faithful and optimistic ones, those who sow ten seeds of faith, blessing and honor for every seed of doubt, cursing and dishonor. Like David and Elisha they see in the Spirit and know the favor of the armies of the Lord of Hosts.

I thought of the scripture that says, "On your walls, O Jerusalem, I have appointed watchmen; all day and all night they will never keep silent. You who remind the Lord, take no rest for yourselves; And give Him no rest until He establishes and makes Jerusalem a praise in the earth." - Isaiah 62:6-7

The man who opened the gate was quite exhausted. It had taken all that was in him, every bit of strength, energy and resolve to reach the gate and trigger the release.

The Spirit said, "I have set apart many for this work, to open the gate and lower the bridge of the Lord for the people. They must find their way out from the castle, which is Hades. The joy of the Lord shall be their strength."

As I thought about this statement, I began to wonder why I first saw a balloon in the hands of the man in the gate and not a banner, but that the balloon then turned into the banner.

The Spirit said, "The difference between the banner and the balloon is that the balloon is filled with the breath of a servant, while the banner is filled with the breath of the King. There is some power in the word of a servant, but much more power is released as a servant learns to proclaim the word of his King. Only the word of the King of heaven and earth can release the power needed to open the gates of Hades completely."

I reasoned that since the Spirit had said this castle represented Hades, the drawbridge must represent the way out. Perhaps this is why the drawbridge seemed so appealing.

THE INVISIBLE IMPASSE

Then I was shown another picture. This time, all the people who were in the gate had begun to cross the drawbridge, but the banner holder was still in the gate, holding the lever open. I was surprised to find out that he was not their leader. This picture only lasted a moment and then I was taken back to the time before they had been released and all the people were still crowded in the gate.

From this it became obvious that the banner holder did not possess the power in himself to lead the people across, but only to mark the way of the exit. Although he had the power to open the gate, and keep it open, so long as he held the banner and the lever simultaneously, he still did not possess the power to make the people cross. He only possessed the power to keep the way open to them. Something else was needed in order for the people to pass. It was as if everyone sensed there was an invisible, impassable threshold that no one would dare to step beyond. This worried me because there was such a desperation and anxiety mounting in the people who crowded in the gate. I myself began to feel weighed down with despair and doubt.

The people looked shifty, frantic and desperate, almost like a prisoner might look in the middle of a prison break. These people were traumatized. Whatever they had been through and wherever they had come from had apparently devastated them. Yet, while they were afraid to move forward, it seemed like no one was willing to fully consider going back. They were trapped between fear and failure, it was as if being in this place of uncertainty was better than being certain in their depravity. But the longer the people had to wait, the more their faith dissipated. The wait was consuming them. I could see their faith, like so many others, was fading as it teetered on the edge of fear and hope. With anxiety and pressure mounting, it did not surprise me when some gave up and began to sink back from the gate and disappear into the belly of the crowd.

The Spirit said, "Perseverance and persistence must increase for your generation to experience their victory over Death."

As he said this, I questioned in my head, "Yes, but it doesn't seem like perseverance and persistence are getting them anywhere. Even those strongest in perseverance seem at most only able to stay at the mouth of the gate—yet never able to cross over."

The Spirit said, "Yes. Perseverance enables one to stay. But few actually do. Perseverance and persistence alone cannot allow anyone to advance any further than they can see or hear. If they are to cross, they must first see and hear."

After the Spirit had said this, I was wondering what it was that they needed to see and hear and what was preventing them from seeing and hearing it.

He said, "They must see and hear Me and they must overcome their fear. Fear of man, fear of death, and fear of failure prevent them from seeing and hearing any further."

The faces of those who stood in the gate expressed fear and terror. Even though no material thing was in their way, no one would dare cross the bridge alone. Fear seemed to create an invisible forcefield at the base of the drawbridge. Everyone imagined there was some trap waiting to trigger on the first person to cross.

Everyone in the gate sensed there was going to be a release, but no one knew when. The anticipation was exciting. But every moment the release didn't come challenged and tested everyone's hope and faith in God. In order to remain in the gate, every last bit of perseverance and persistence was needed.

Through all of this, one thing became clear: something needed to happen. The circumstances needed to change if they were going to escape their past and move forward.

THE GLORIOUS WHITE HORSE

I looked in frustration and sadness as the multitude of people smashed together into the gate. I wanted to yell at them to stay strong and to persevere, but I couldn't encourage them, for I also could not see any hope for their deliverance. Though I searched my imagination for any scenario that could free them, all I could imagine was their doom. How could I encourage them if I myself had no hope for them.

The Spirit spoke, "Hope belongs only to those who can see what is not yet visible."

Hearing Him say this, I looked back to the crowd of people. How was I supposed to see what was not visible? I squinted in attempt to see anything different than before. All I could see was the same hopeless situation. The situation had to change if they would have any hope.

The Spirit said, "Faith is no companion to that which is now visible. Those who have eyes to see let them see what the Spirit says to the churches."

After a moment, He spoke again, "Faith offends the eye. That is unless you have exchanged your natural eyes for spiritual ones. You must see in spirit to walk in spirit."

I remembered what it says in Romans 10:17, "Faith is the assurance of things hoped for, the conviction of things not seen." I thought to myself, "This is saying that living by faith is living as if future hopes are certainties and unseen things are realities."

I snapped back. Looking to the crowd, I still didn't see anything. How could I see the unseen? How would they be delivered?

The Spirit then suddenly announced with a loud voice, "Behold, the Great White Horse!"

Near the front of the gate, a beautiful, strong, white horse began to emerge and make his way to the front of the multitude. This horse was very happy and very strong, excited like a dog when his owner first comes home from a long trip. Yet it was not we who owned him. There was something beyond the gate that he was fixed upon. Everyone seemed to know this horse somehow carried their deliverance in his vision. His eyes carried a steadfast focus that completely contradicted the wavering, hopelessness and fear that governed the atmosphere of the crowd at the gate. He had a type of confidence and authority that inspired a different type of fear. His eyes scanned the horizon, looking right through anything in its path. He was seeing something no one else was able to see. It was a reverent fear that arose in all who saw him. It almost felt like shame. Standing next to him, we were all stricken by a knowledge of how we should be, but are not. It was the type of fear that comes when you see one who must make up for your own weakness. Knowing that all hope for life and freedom rests in his mercy and in his power.

The Holy Spirit said, "His name is Faith."

Moving steadily forward, all eyes were locked on him as he grew closer to the threshold which no one had dared cross before. What would he do when he got to the place we all could not pass? What would he do with the weight of speculation and fear? As he reached the line, he crossed the invisible barrier without any change in his pace or vision. It was shockingly uneventful. His utter unconcern for everyone's invisible, impassable threshold made everyone feel like superstitious fools.

"You see what holds the world back?" The Spirit said. "So many of your barriers and limits are only illusions that are moved by mere faith, or the lack thereof. All of your impossibilities don't even exist."

I remembered the scripture, "With man this is impossible, but with God all things are possible." - Matthew 19:26

And, "For nothing will be impossible with God." - Luke 1:37

I too felt ridiculous for my superstition. As the people in the gate saw him cross the bridge, their hearts were released to run red again. Fiery boldness filled them and in one accord they lunged forward out of the castle's gate. The sight of it was powerful! With so much united movement and force, it was like a dam had just been breached as the flood of humanity poured out behind the horse. The horse began to lead what now looked like a great parade with music and shouts of triumph up the path on the hill on which I was standing.

OPPOSITION TO THE BANNER OF JOY

In the next picture, the man with the banner was still in the entrance of the gate, holding the gate lever open. Again, I thought how odd it was that he was not the first in line behind the white horse. As he was standing there, holding the gate open, another man came up who had a big stone slate. He began using it to try to cover and squash the gatekeeper and his banner.

Because the gatekeeper's hands were both being used to hold the banner and the gate's lever, the man with the stone slate had an open target and was taking full swings and smashing him on his head time and time again with the stone slate. Each time his head was pounded, it hurt as one might imagine, but it seemed like the blows didn't have the power to make him weak or even to break or bruise his skin.

The Spirit said, "Beware of the religious man."

Then I was taken inside the castle walls. Here I could see the gate as one looking out from inside. I was surprised to see that very few of the people on this side seemed to know there was even a gate or exit at all. They were just blindly being pushed about by the swirl of the crowd. While the crowds couldn't necessarily see the exit, what they could see was the banner. It's colors stood out in stark contrast to the grey stone walls of the castle. And while they could not guess the banner marked the exit, there was yet something about it that drew them to it. Many of the people were making it their aim. Because of this, there was a great amount of dependency upon the man with the banner. The job of this banner holder was crucial. If he gave up, or if the man who was hitting him with the stone slate was able to cause him to fall, there would be little hope if any in finding the exit at all.

It surprised me to see that no one was coming to the aid of the one who held the banner. His role was so essential, and he was being pummeled by the man with the stone slate, yet no one seemed to even notice or care. Once the people got to him and his banner, not one of them offered to help. In fact, they all seemed to forget about the banner altogether as soon as they could see for themselves the skies of open freedom and the white horse that led their procession.

The Holy Spirit said, "He is a standard bearer."

The man in the gate was learning what it was to be a standard bearer for the Lord.

The Spirit continued, "A standard bearer carries the flag and symbol of another, for the praise and glory of another. To this one his strength and his joy is not dependent upon his earthly consequences, but upon his King's reign."

Now, as I looked with great respect at the standard bearer, the Spirit allowed me to see his thoughts. He longed so badly to be with the horse at the front of the crowd—not because he was ambitious to lead, but because he thought that the people at the front would be the first to see the King and enter His domain. In his mind, this crowd of people were his kinsmen, on exodus from the captivity of a false kingdom in search of the kingdom to which they belonged. As he watched person after person go by, many of them seemed to take for granted the blessings of the place they were headed. It would have been hard for any man not to become bitter in this place. He would have if it were not for the joy of the Lord and the nearness of his heart to God, who led him to love these people so deeply. Yet he often wondered why God had chosen him to stay and fight this man with the stone slate and hold the gate for people who never seemed to notice. He had so many reasons to fail, yet in all of this he never allowed the banner of joy to drop.

Through this it seemed like the Spirit wanted to show me that if one is called to carry the banner of joy and hold the gate for the Lord and His people, they must know that they will have to fight to keep that banner up and they will often feel completely alone. It will not be for any earthly recognition or kingdom. In fact they will have to forfeit their own kingdom and wait until the very end to see their reward and enter the things promised.

The Spirit said, "He is learning what it is to be one of the least in the Kingdom of heaven."

Chapter 2

The Castle of Religious Law

NEXT I WAS TAKEN UP ABOVE the castle. From this vantage point I could see that the castle was much longer than I had first thought. The entire castle was asymmetrical. There were multi-level platforms and thousands of walled off divisions throughout the castle. On each platform and in each room there were multitudes of people. It was a mess. Everything looked like it had been built, rebuilt, torn down, and re-erected on top of itself many times. I imagined that it would be hard to find a place to rest on the cold, crowded grey stones that these floors and walls were made of. I couldn't think of any reason why anyone would choose to stay in this place unless they had no other choice.

I also saw that if you were walking into the stone castle from outside through the drawbridge, you would first come into a large, square courtyard at ground level. The large wall surrounding the courtyard was about 15 feet wide and made a pathway which overlooked both the courtyard and the area outside the castle. This was the type of wall that was built to provide its occupants an advantage against an attack. Originally I thought that the whole castle was merely the size of this courtyard, but actually it was hundreds, if not thousands of times larger. There were multitudes of other rooms and levels that made up the castle. Each level had small stairways going up or down to other nearby levels.

Although there were people everywhere, there were particularly high concentrations of people at the stairways. There were many people currently building levels higher and higher. It took me a moment to realize that most of the people in the castle were trying to move to higher levels rather than lower ones. Many more people were trying to go up the narrow stairways than down. This made it very difficult to pass from level to level especially for those going down. This was interesting because the lowest place in the whole castle was the courtyard with the gate that seemed to be the only way out. Many people would have to travel against the flow down many stairways to get to this place.

The Spirit said, "The exit from Hades is found only at its lowest place. To leave this place, they must first come down out of their high places. The name of the courtyard floor is Humility. Humility must be found if anyone from this place is to see the Kingdom of God."

The castle itself was very long. My eyes scanned the distance of the castle until they found the opposite end, where I could see a second exit from the castle. At the front end, one could exit by coming down into the courtyard, through the gate, and over the drawbridge. This is what I had seen happening with the procession at the beginning. At the opposite end, a second exit went into a graveyard. The river which began at the front of the castle under the drawbridge flowed rapidly in both directions around the castle and ended at the back of the castle where the water was being siphoned and sucked into the tombs of the graveyard.

The Spirit pointed me to the drawbridge on the one end and then to the graveyard at the other end. He said, "The name of the one is Life, the other, Death."

The only way out of this castle was by life or by death. I saw many of the residents of the castle throwing dead bodies into the graveyard which was the doorway of death.

From the aerial view, one could see a distant ocean beyond the castle. From the ocean, waves of fire-like liquid were coming and washing through the graveyard behind the castle. The graveyard was never able to keep its dead, for each time a set of waves swept though, the dead bodies would be swept out to sea. The waves seemed to be cleansing the tombs of the dead. These were not like normal waves, but more like tidal waves. There were three separate waves that came in.

The Spirit said, "Waves to wash away all things unwritten."

I thought of the scripture in Revelation that speaks of the New Jerusalem. It says, "Nothing unclean, and no one who practices abomination and lying, shall ever come into it, but only those whose names are written in the Lamb's book of life." –Revelation 21:27

In the graveyard at the end of the rivers, sometimes you could not see the tombstones because the water level was too high. All you could see was a funnel of water sucking down at tomb's location. At other times you could see the tombstones. It seemed that the depth and the current were dependent on the weight of the castle. I realized that the island might not be as much of an island as it was a type of boat. The heavier the castle got, the more the island would sink.

At this time, even though I knew the castle represented Hades, I asked the Spirit if the castle had a name.

He said, "Its name is "Man's Law." It is made of the yeast of the Pharisees."

From this I had a convincing sense that the Spirit didn't just mean that the castle was built on a few of man's laws, but on all of man's laws. It included all of man's religious laws, his ideological laws, and even his social laws. Each stone brick within the castle represented another religion, belief, ideology, government or law into which people placed their security and identity. Together, these stone bricks would make up rooms, levels and walls that held together the complete world views of the people within each room.

There were rooms and layers that were built to emphasize political, philosophical, and social ideologies. But most of all, rooms were built to emphasize religious ideologies. Many rooms and layers emphasized a combination of ideologies.

For the first time, I noticed how foggy and hazy it was in the castle. The entire structure had a thick fog covering it, making it hard for anyone to see. Some floors were more foggy then others. The people who existed on these platforms knew that there were other platforms out there, but instead of having an honest curiosity about them they only seemed to fear them. So long as their circumstances permitted, most of the people within each level were content only to know that their own level existed and was secure. The thought of other levels only brought insecurity to them. The people within these walls always seemed to carry around the fear that if they didn't pay close attention to the bricks on their own floor, they would not know where their level ended and they could easily end up falling right off of it.

Within the castle, all movement and access was dictated by the laws that made up each floor. Because of this, the people were always bent over, looking at the floor, to make sure they were not violating any of their laws. At first I thought they were just doing this so that they could see the ground better, but then I realized that many of the people within the castle were actually bent over because they had severe hunchbacks. They couldn't straighten out even if they wanted to. Because the fog made it so hard to see and the people had to focus so intently on the bricks below them, every generation that passed by caused them to evolve more and more into a race of hunchbacks.

Even though it was hard to see, I could make out what seemed to be different banners that were held on each level that represented the chief ideology of the room. I found a small one that said, "CAPITALIST" another small one said, "COMMUNIST." There were thousands upon thousands of levels, many overlapping, and many intersecting. I saw many that were built upon others and others that had been destroyed. One smaller one said, "REPUBLICAN," another one said, "LIBERAL." I saw a large and growing floor named, "ISLAM." From this floor rose other floors, "SUNNI" and "SHIITE" were some of them. I saw another large level named "HINDUISM." There were many, many floors that rose from this one. There were many floors with names I had never seen before.

There was one base level that weaved and ran almost the entire base of the island. It is the floor that almost all these others were built upon. At first I couldn't see its banner. But later it emerged and its name was "HUMANISM." The procession was a procession out from these false laws, religions and structures of man.

MAN'S KNOWLEDGE

Next, the Spirit showed me one of the levels that man had built for himself in the castle. It was a huge level.

The Spirit said, "One of the largest today."

It was interesting that it was pretty low compared to many other levels. It had a direct stairway to the courtyard wall where the drawbridge was. The people on this level in particular were very good at inspecting the bricks in front of them. They were excellent at defining where they lived.

The Spirit said, "Truly these are the seed of Adam. Naming and defining is what they do as Adam did in the garden. This is enjoyable to the Lord. But these also like Adam are lovers of the fruit of knowledge. The only difference between them and Adam is they care not for the fruit of the knowledge of good and evil, but just of knowledge."

Man's knowledge, natural law and science seemed to be the bricks that they used to give themselves security and to determine the perimeter of their reality. Even though they had no ceiling and they could see the heavens plainly, they refused to accept that anything outside of the confines of their floor could be true. They only accepted the things that they understood and could define. These ones embraced and loved their own hunchbacks.

Some of these could see a stairway that led beyond their level. There were also a few here who looked up for a time and saw the great light that was above and outside of their room. To them, this light was without measure on both sides. They couldn't see the end of it. Therefore, they could not admit it as part of their floor. Because their law was their god, they were forced to deny the source of the very light they used to see. They determined only to relate to the light to the extent that they could measure its effects on their level, their law. They didn't create the light that they used to establish understanding. Yet they used their understanding to disregard the source of their light.

"They will be judged for this." The Spirit said. "So many will be surprised at the judgment."

He continued, "Too much exposure to light will always destroy things that have been living in darkness. Too much exposure to darkness will always destroy things made to thrive in light. Yet while things of darkness are destroyed by light, things of light are not destroyed by darkness in and of itself, but they are destroyed for lack of light. Darkness is truly only an absence of light—whether in the spirit or in the body. Darkness is able to exist in light, but not over any extended amount of time. The root of darkness is ignorance. Darkness has no power but ignorance. As soon as it is exposed to light, it immediately begins to recede and break down. But, if its residue and its corpse are not buried or cleaned up, many will assume and live as if darkness were still there with all its former power."

Even though I could not see a banner for this level, I assumed that it would have been named, "Objectivism," or "Science," or "Man's Knowledge," or "Modernism," or "Absolutism" or something along these lines.

THE OFFSPRING OF MANS KNOWLEDGE

There was second level in the dead center of the level of man's knowledge. The level of man's knowledge seemed to be pregnant with this one, but this level was lower down. It was very low, very humble, but it seemed to be merely a kind of pretend humility, a false humility, because the only way to it or from it was from its higher level. There is no release; no progress from that place to anywhere else unless you first go back to the level of man's knowledge.

"What is that level?" I asked.

Then I heard faint whispers speaking words like desperation, compromise, false ideologies. I realized that if the previous, higher level truly represented "Objectivism," "Absolutism" and "Modernism," this lower level must represent "Subjectivism," "Relativism" and "Post-modernism." The people on this floor claimed to be free from all law, especially religious law, but in doing so, they established their own law, their own religion. This religion was not based on truth though, but upon a rebellion against truth. This little mini courtyard that descended from modernism was just a drug that numbed all reason. It was defined by what started with a search for truth alone, but ended with a denial of objective reason, unless it served a personal subjective purpose.

Chapter 3

Christianity & its Antichrist

THERE WAS ANOTHER LARGE FLOOR—one of the largest of all. It's name was "CHRISTIANITY." Like Hinduism, there were also many different floors that arose out of this one. This greatly alarmed me because I had assumed the Christians were the ones I had seen escaping from the castle and heading up into the forest.

The Spirit said, "Many of those who call themselves Christian are on Moses' wall. They can see Christ, but they have never gone through the courtyard or the doorway. They are those who have become content to see with limited revelation so long as they are not personally affected, confronted or broken by it. These are the types who would have a hard time receiving the good things that can be found in a revelation like this. They are legalistic. They love the scripture for its security and answers, not as much for its Author. All works without relationship are vain religion. The Church is not somewhere you go to, it is someone you are. It is not the people who go to church, but the people who are the Church who will enter the kingdom of God."

I saw a great separation of those who are Moses Christians and those in the procession.

The Spirit continued, "The Kingdom of God is not about bringing the supernatural back into the natural, but bringing the natural back into the supernatural. It is not God who needs to move—God is constant—it is you who must move."

He continued, "When you set up laws to enforce or emphasize anything but Christ alone, it is folly. Those who do are still seeing as one in the castle. Calling yourself a Christian doesn't necessarily mean you are a follower of Christ. It matters only who you place your security in, who you place your identity in, who you obey and why."

As I looked I found virtually every Christian organization that I could imagine. I found big general levels that many others were built upon. I saw three main levels named, "ROMANISM," "ORTHODOX," and "LUTHERANISM" (I believe Lutheranism would include all of Protestantism), which were intersected and divided by two others named "CHRISTIAN-LIBERAL," and "CHRISTIAN-CONSERVATIVE." Upon these foundations I saw many other levels that were built and were now flying the banner of their own celebrated denomination, division or ideology.

I was surprised also to see that two of the fastest growing levels with the most workers were named "PENTECOSTAL" and "CHARISMATIC." I was surprised because again, I had assumed that Hades had no room for "CHRISTIANITY." Once I learned it did, then I subconsciously thought it was probably only the "Spirit-filled" churches that were in the procession. I was wrong.

The Spirit spoke, "Hades only offers a place to those who give place to Hades. It is not that Hades has made room for Christianity, but that Christianity has made room for Hades. That's why many of them are here. It's not that Hades has made a place for Pentecostals, Charismatics, Protestants, Orthodox or Catholics, but that many Pentecostals, Charismatics, Protestants, Orthodox and Catholics have made a place for Hades."

THE ANTICHRIST & THE CHRIST

At this point I became a little nauseous—I was now beginning to feel what the Spirit had said. Your title and association means nothing unless it is Christ. I couldn't help but think of how much work I had done to brand and market my ministry. I thought about how so much of our church work in the west is about branding and marketing. I considered how easy it is for us to replace Christ with our brands and create divisions in our hearts against all who are not in our brand.

"Antichrist." I heard the Spirit say.

"Antichrist?" I thought to myself, "How does the antichrist have anything to do with this."

The Spirit replied, "You do not understand."

He continued, "You think of antichrist as a man but I tell you that he is a spirit. And his spirit is not one—he is many. He divides and is divided all over the world. In every place, he seeks to replace Christ."

He continued, "Antichrist is a spirit who denies the work of Christ and in its place promotes the work of man. He especially hates that Christ became man for in His humanity, Christ revealed man as divine. He revealed God as your Father—that your image and likeness is His image and likeness."

He paused for a moment, but before I could sort through what was being said, He continued. "Antichrist cares not what Christ is replaced with, but only that Christ is replaced. He loves to label "christian" everything that does not reveal Christ. He turns the cross into anything that will keep people from experiencing the union that Christ purchased. He denies Christ in you. Instead, he teaches that Christ is only in a few. He sells costly stairways to help people reach God even though God has already offered Himself to you freely at His own expense. He teaches that you are so dirty that you could never assume to commune with God. He loves to replace the revelation of Christ in you with the revelation of religion in you. He convinces the house of God to believe lies about the image and works of Christ, and therefore about their own image and works."

He continued, partially quoting Jesus from Matthew 23:13-15, "Woe to the scribes and Pharisees who are hypocrites! They have shut the kingdom of heaven in people's faces. For they neither enter the Kingdom themselves nor do they allow those who would enter to go in. Woe to the hypocrites who travel across sea and land to make a single proselyte, and when he becomes a proselyte, they make him twice as much a child of hell as they are."

My mind was racing. I thought of God's house, His temple, and about all the big name denominational leaders and tele-evangelists that the Spirit must be talking about.

The Spirit spoke loudly, "You are God's temple."

I was shocked. He was talking about me—about all of us, about Christianity. I was overwhelmed by the thought of how often I operated in the spirit of the antichrist. I wondered how pure my motives had been. Had I just been selling methods and formulas? Was I thinking of others as if God was far from them? Was I thinking of people as if they were not made in His image and likeness–as if in His eyes, they were not also His children?

After a time of examining myself and allowing my conscience to be cleansed, my mind returned to the idea of the antichrist. I had always thought the antichrist would be a charismatic world leader who would stand in the temple in Jerusalem and bring peace to the middle east for three and a half years, but would end up persecuting the Church and bringing world war. The Spirit, at least in this encounter, seemed to be saying that antichrist has already come, and has already been infiltrating the Church and each of us personally.

I looked up the word "antichrist" in the scriptures and found only four references; all of which are in the epistles of first and second John.

"Children, it is the last hour, and as you have heard that antichrist is coming, so now many antichrists have come. Therefore we know that it is the last hour." - 1 John 2:18

"Who is the liar but he who denies that Jesus is the Christ? This is the antichrist, he who denies the Father and the Son." - 1 John 2:22

"Every spirit that does not confess Jesus is not from God. This is the spirit of the antichrist, which you heard was coming and now is in the world already." 1 John 4:3

"For many deceivers have gone out into the world, those who do not confess the coming of Jesus Christ in the flesh. Such a one is the deceiver and the antichrist." - 2 John 1:7

As I read these passages, I thought to myself, "I guess I didn't really understand antichrist."

The Spirit answered, "Neither have you fully understood Christ."

He continued, "Christ is both God and man. The name Christ is the name into which we have all merged. The flesh of men and the Spirit of God are one in the body of Messiah. You are one, because We are One. The antichrist is he who opposes the dignity deserved for the image of God and union of Christ in all of humanity. He opposes the union Christ accomplished when He became human flesh."

I thought of the passage that says, "And the Word became flesh, and dwelt among us, and we saw His glory, glory as of the only begotten from the Father, full of grace and truth... For the Law was given through Moses; grace and truth were realized through Jesus Christ." - John 1:14,17

He continued, "Just as Christ is the revelation of God, He is also the revelation of man. Just as He is the definition of God, He is also the definition of man. He is divine and He is flesh. He married the two. In Him, God and Man are One. He reconciled the two. Do you not understand what it means for man to have an ambassador—a representative? The identity of man has been wrapped up into Christ. Christ has consumed you. He now defines you.

I had the sense that He was talking not just about me, but about the entire human race. But how could this be? How could He define all of us when so many of us act so wickedly?

"Yes," the Spirit affirmed, "Just as in Noah, the race of man was saved, even though many perished, so too in Christ the race of man is saved even though many perish. Christ is the ark of man's salvation. In Christ, man is shown holy, even though many still perish in their wickedness. In Christ, man is shown innocent, even though many still perish with a guilty conscience. In Christ, man is shown worthy, even though many still perish for lack of dignity. In Christ, man is shown to possess all authority, even though many still perish from bondage."

His words were striking a chord deep within my soul. I felt like I could explode with joy and sorrow simultaneously. What was said was so beautiful and good, but I was having a hard time accepting it all.

"This is My message." The Spirit said, "It is a finished work. Their sins are forgiven. Their debts are paid. I have reconciled them back to Myself, not as a result of their own works, but of Mine. I restored them to their original state which is My image and My likeness. It is true that many are not currently experiencing the grace of this truth. They must hear the message of Christ in order to experience the truth. Those who have not heard the message of Christ are not yet experiencing the benefits of My salvation. They are still caught up in their sin. Most of them are still living in Adam—on the island of isolation."

THE KINGDOM OF GOD & THE KINGDOMS OF MEN

After some time, my eyes returned once again to the castle and to the floor of Christianity. I could see that the people on these floors had come to identify themselves, define themselves and place their security more in the laws that made up their floor than in Christ. At this point I had become very frightened for the church and for myself.

I asked the Spirit, "Are all of those who fellowship within these denominations, brands and segregations not going to make it into Your Kingdom?"

The Spirit said, "No, they may. It is only those within these floors who have taken their laws and are now holding them up as a filter between themselves and Christ and between themselves and each other that cannot fully see My Kingdom. For My Kingdom is in the midst of all of them. Yet even now I am not against them, I am for them. I come to them to draw them out to Me. And unless they come out from this idolatry, it will be very difficult for them to see or enter the kingdom of God.

I thought of the passage that says, "Nor will they say, 'Look, here it is!' or 'There!' for behold, the Kingdom of God is in the midst of you." - Luke 17:21

After a moment He spoke with a softer tone, "But you do not understand what it is to see or enter My Kingdom."

He continued, "When you think of entering the Kingdom you think of a future date. When I think of you entering the Kingdom I think of a present, full embrace. I think of every time you choose to embrace the union between you and your Creator and Father. Seeing and entering the Kingdom of God has as much to do with your present faith as it does with anything in the past or the future. It is the same with salvation and sanctification. Death is not your savior. Nor is it your sanctifier. Christ is. Salvation is wherever and whenever Christ is. Sanctification is wherever and whenever Christ is. And the Kingdom of God is wherever and whenever Christ is. Do you believe? Do you believe that My Kingdom is at hand? Do you believe that it is no longer you who live but Christ who lives in you?

He continued, "But indeed, many will not believe My dominion today and so they will not see or enter My dominion today."

Again, after some time, my eyes returned to the castle levels. So many of the people were studying and caring for their bricks.

The Spirit said, "Fallen man finds his security and identity in letters and laws. Risen man finds his security and identity in Me alone. For the risen man, My law is not burdensome, nor will it by itself give security or identity—but merely opportunity. And I write My law on the tablet of his heart, not on the tablets of stone."

As He said this, I thought of how much security and identity I had placed in the laws and ideologies of man. The evidence for my idolatry was the fact that I was threatened and took personal offense if an attack was made on any one of my social, philosophical, political, or religious ideologies. It was as if an attack on them was the same as a personal attack on me.

The Spirit said, "You have allowed these a place on the throne of your heart. Christ alone belongs there."

I thought of all the times I had become defensive and argued against people—not for the sake of the truth or with a genuine consideration, but because my security and identity were being threatened and because I had come to place my security and identity into the success of my ideologies.

Growing up as a republican I had come to hate liberals because they came from a different level then I did and I didn't know if they had the power to destroy my level. In my heart, my level was more important than them. Thus, I chose to fight them at all costs because their mere presence was a threat to the level that I had come to know and trust. Thinking back I can say that all along I could hear the Spirit saying that He loves them just as much as He loves me.

The Lord began to show me that there were many liberals who had great godly motives for being liberal. Yet still, the vast majority of them could not see that a republican could have great and godly motives too. The vast majority of republicans were also blinded to seeing the liberals' motives. In regard to politics, many were first a republican, then a follower of Christ. Likewise, many were first a liberal, then a follower of Christ. Because of this, the person was completely blind to the hatred and prejudice they had toward the other party regardless of Christ's love for them. This was total darkness and idolatry. I felt ashamed for all the times I had practiced blind and prejudiced hatred towards people. I thought of all the times I had failed to seek out the good in others, to love others, and to hope the best in others.

My identity and security had been totally wrapped up in the success of these ideologies. I realized that placing my identity and security in anything other than Christ was faulty. I thought about how much destruction had come into the world and how many relationships had been broken because people had placed their security and identity into manmade ideologies. It amazed me how so many of us would rather defend our ideologies at the cost of life and love than to see them lost.

At this time I realized it wasn't just outward ideologies that had become idols of false security and identity. I had been subject to a large number of inward ideologies and false securities. I thought of how much security I placed in my own ability to pastor a church. If there was not a big crowd, then in my heart it reflected on me personally and it revealed some kind of failure or disapproval. If ministry was growing and doing well, then I was secure. I thought that I was successful in God's eyes if I were growing a ministry. My identity in my heart was wrapped up in the success of the church. I was beginning to see this was faulty. I am secure in Christ alone because of His work upon the cross.

The Spirit said, "Popularity defines the success of many of those who don't know their Father. Contentment is a trait of all those who have truly received the revelation of Christ. Only from this place can you begin to fathom the type of gain that heaven considers true."

I remembered the passage that says, "Godliness actually is a means of great gain when accompanied by contentment." -1 Tim 6:6

In the context of this passage, Paul was referring to those who were in ministry for worldly gain and popularity. He was saying that true "gain" in the Kingdom cannot be accomplished without contentment.

All this made me think that I might not truly know my Father. I assumed that I had come to know God because I had come to know the scriptures. Yet in my heart, all along I knew there was an infinite amount of God I had not yet come close to.

I thought of the scripture in which Jesus says to the Jews, "You search the Scriptures because in them you think you have eternal life; it is these that testify about Me; and you are unwilling to come to Me so that you may have life." -John 5:39-40.

The Spirit said, "The Scriptures were never meant to be a replacement for God. They were meant only to be the testimony and witness of what you could have and experience with God."

After a few minutes, my mind began to wonder about the verses in Hebrews 13:17 and Romans 13:1 that command us to submit to the governing authorities and how this would obviously involve the laws of man. So I thought to myself, "All law isn't bad is it? Even if it is only man's law God still commands us to obey it so it must be good."

The Spirit said, "Yes, I command you to submit to the laws of man, but in the beginning it was not this way. In the beginning there was God. This is what I came to restore to you."

I remembered how the scriptures say that the law only came in to increase the testimony of sin that we might be brought to Christ (Romans 3:19-20; 5:20-21).

The Spirit said, "I will honor the laws of man, and I will repay every lawless deed. Yet there is one law that overrules all others. This law is the one by which all others will be judged. It is the Law of Love."

He continued, "When there is true love, there is no need for any law besides it. This is what I meant when I said that in the beginning there was only God. In the beginning there was only relationship, there was only love."

This was hard for me to comprehend. It was hard for me to believe that I was hearing the Holy Spirit. I thought, "No laws in society? That sounds like anarchy. I don't think anarchy is what God wants."

The Spirit replied, "No. Anarchy means no one rules. The Kingdom of God means God's absolute rule. It is not that there is no law or rule, but the opposite. It is that the one absolute law and King have complete dominance over all. Idolatry is when security and identity is placed in any object other than your Father."

I spent some time thinking about all that had been said. I thought about how all the early churches in the book of Acts just referred to themselves as the church of it's city. There were no brands or denominations. Maybe this is how it was meant to be, but I couldn't imagine any denomination wanting to return to this. Every church I know of has a name. If they dropped their names it might send every church into an identity crisis. But maybe that is not such a bad thing. I began wondering whether church naming in general was just another tactic of the evil one. I still couldn't say that I had a clear answer. So I asked the Spirit, "Does branding our ministries work contrary to the Kingdom of God.

He answered, "Branding, like many mortal inventions, is neutral. It is the hearts of men that make things holy or defiled."

I thought to myself that branding is merely a marketing term, a strategy for bringing definition and clarity to a product in order to gain traffic and create business.

"But be careful," the Spirit said, "Branding and defining promotes comparison and for this reason it is in its nature to bring division. This is not My strategy for My Church. Branding defines its object in contrast to others while Christ defines Himself in union with others. He became man. He united himself with your flesh that you might unite with His divinity."

"So do you want us all to drop our church names?" I questioned.

"It is not branding that brings division, but the jealousy, fear, envy and strife that are within peoples hearts. Whether or not a church brands itself is something every church leader should receive from Me. Yet, do not harden your heart or entertain thoughts of speculation or accusation against anyone who has a brand or does not have a brand. Leave judgment to Me for man sees not as I see; for man looks at outward appearances but I look at the heart."

He said further, "Not all structure and law is bad, but in order to build the Kingdom of God, no man can lay a foundation other than the One which is laid, which is Jesus Christ. (1 Cor. 3:11) This castle represents all that has been built upon something other than the person of Christ. It represents all that has been built upon the island of isolation and separation from God. It represents all things built or sustained without Him as head and forerunner. He alone is the author of all true life and light."

Chapter 4

The Courtyard
& the Stone Man

NEXT I WAS TAKEN AGAIN to the first view where I could see the front of the castle. This time, a multitude of dark figures were standing on the castle wall above the courtyard. The impression I had from the beginning was that it was not a peaceful atmosphere, but that it was an atmosphere of war. Because of this, I expected those who stood above the courtyard on the castle wall to be shooting arrows or dumping tar on the people who were escaping by crossing the drawbridge below, but they were not. Instead, they were all turned inward, distracted by something else that was inside the courtyard of the castle.

The dark figures who walked on the walls of Hades were intimidating, but they were not necessarily enemies. They all seemed independent of each other. They were sad or perhaps apathetic, but they did not seem hostile. I sensed a change of emotion in the Spirit. As He focused on them, He seemed to see them for who they would be, could be, and should be if living without restraint and given open freedom. He became mournful.

He said, "They are stolen from Me."

THE WORD OF GOD

Then I was brought inside the courtyard. It had a single large, stone stairway which started in the dead-center of the courtyard and rose up to the rim of the wall opposite of the gate. There I saw what the dark multitude was concerned with.

On the single stairway was a great huge stone man, about 12 feet tall, and about 10 feet wide. It looked like He was made of shiny silver stone. At first sight, He startled me and brought fear to me. But then I thought to myself that I shouldn't fear because I am on His side.

The Holy Spirit said, "Actually, it is He who is on your side. He is actually on everyone's side. It is not He who needs a defender; it is you who need a defender. It is not He who is confused about who He is, and what He is and where He is. It is you who knows not and sees not and hears not your purpose, your value."

I looked at the stone giant. He was uncompromising. He was unyielding. He was fearless and awful. He would not be bothered or stopped by anyone for anything. He had a type of unstoppable motivation that drove intimidation into all that looked on him. He did not care to converse. There was no negotiating with Him. He had one objective with every one that He encountered.

The Spirit said, "His name is 'The Word of God.'"

I was startled by His name. I thought about how the Spirit had said earlier that He was on everyone's side. How could the word of God be on everyone's side? What about those who disobey the word of God? Is the word of God still on their side?

The Spirit said, "You do not know the true nature of the Word of God. You are still seeing the Word of God as through the lens of Hades. If you, and they, (He motioned to the people in the castle) could only behold Him as He truly is! Only then would you know yourself as you truly are."

Even though I could not see the Holy Spirit, it was as if He had been standing next to me this whole time and at this point He seemed to move directly in front of me as if standing face to face with me. I could feel His eyes burning into mine. I could not stand it any longer and so I closed my eyes. I heard Him speak again, "If you will look through my eye, I will reveal His Nature in you."

I opened my eyes and was shocked to see that the Spirit had swooped me up and placed me directly behind the stone giant. I was now hovering about 2 feet behind His massive back. My immediate reaction was to try to get away, but my second thought was curiosity. What was His true nature?

I looked at this massive hulk and saw that in the shiny silver stone that made up His body, there were hundreds, or thousands of mirrored surfaces, each reflecting something different. It looked as if there were hundreds of TV screens of all shapes and sizes, all showing videos of different things. It was like each surface was enchanted. As I focused on a smaller parallelogram shaped surface in His lower back, I was drawn in and saw a tree whose roots were growing and spreading across the surface of the ground. I then saw a seed some distance away. The roots grew over and began to cover the seed. I could tell the roots were not intending to harm the seed, but to save it, to nurture it and to cause it to grow. The movie slowed down in such a way to suggest that something crucial was just revealed. But as I began to reflect on what it could mean, my eyes were drawn to another screen where I saw a young man holding hundreds of keys standing in a corridor with many doors. As he used his keys to open the doors, he could not value the treasure he found in the rooms because he knew not how to read the names on the doors. Again it slowed down as if to invite me to reflect on the magnitude of what he had just said but the Spirit yanked me back and all of a sudden I was aware of myself again.

Each screen was so beautiful; the colors were brilliant. It was surreal. Each surface had such a pull to it that it was impossible not to get lost in the fascination of each revelation. I could feel myself forgetting about time and matter. It was like each screen revealed a truth and a beauty so deep it would take a lifetime to discover the depths of it.

At this point the stone giant suddenly turned so his face was directly in front of mine, "I know who you truly are. I alone. I can reveal who you truly are. I alone."

As I hovered there in awe, the Spirit continued, "What you saw in Him is what He sees in you. He did not come to show people who they are not, but who they truly are. Can you see now? His work is not to judge people, but to reveal them. Judgment is merely a by-product of an unveiled heart. Everyone will be judged, but you are not ready for judgment yet because you have not yet seen yourself completely in Him. He waits in this place, desiring to reveal every last one who would come to Him."

I was also reminded of the scripture that says, "For the word of God is quick, and powerful, and sharper than any two-edged sword, piercing even to the dividing asunder of soul and spirit, and of the joints and marrow, and is a discerner of the thoughts and intents of the heart. Neither is there any creature hidden from his sight: but all things are naked and opened unto the eyes of him with whom we have to do." (Hebrews 4:12-13)

CONFRONTING THE STONE MAN

The only way down into the courtyard was through the stone giant. I could see no other way. There was a constant flow of all kinds of different people who came to Him. The response of the stone giant was the same for every person who approached. He would grab them anyway He could, look at them in the eye for a second, and hurl them way up and over his head and they would come crashing down and land about 30 feet behind him on the floor of the courtyard. A few seconds later, someone else would come up, he would grab them and do the same—over and over again.

I wondered why on a surface level, anyone from Hades would want to have an encounter with Him. I could see that some mustered up the courage because they saw justice in Him. They thought that even though their bodies were destined to be broken by the stone giant, somehow they would end up better and freer for it. Some saw hope in Him, and some sought to fight Him. Others just ended up there without purposing to do so.

If you were standing on the castle wall looking down into the courtyard, you could not see a gate or an exit because there was a blinding light that shown upwards from where the gate of the castle was. In addition, there was a heavy fog in the courtyard that made everything hard to see. Once the stone giant threw someone down there, they'd disappear and you'd never see them come back up again. Seeing this helped me understand why the people in the gate whom I saw earlier had such a hard time seeing any exit at all.

Then I was taken down to the floor level of the courtyard. There I saw one of the men who had been thrown by the stone giant. When he hit the ground, he, along with his clothing and all, was broken into thousands of pieces, just like a clay pot or a crystal vase might look if it was smashed on the ground. In this case, as soon as the man was broken, he was also instantly put back together. He was being broken from the rigidity of the castle.

The Spirit said, "Shells of hardness must be broken off. Hearts of stone must become hearts of flesh once again."

I watched as he was being remade; his new body looked almost identical to his old one except without a hunchback. He remained there lying naked and still until his body was completely remade. Then he began to awaken.

Chapter 5

The People of the Court

AS THE MAN AWOKE, he found himself lying there naked with a bright light shining all around him. He looked up and saw something like a bright star, or perhaps a diamond, but made of light. It was exceedingly bright and brilliant, like the sun. Yet it was only about fifteen or twenty feet away from him. He looked at it once, then squinted and covered his eyes as if his eyes lacked the power to look at it a second time. It was a virgin's light. You could behold it once, but once you looked, it did something to your eyes. You could never see anything in it's former light again. All lesser lights were now dimmed and dark when seen with the eyes that had looked on the great light. I was reminded of the white horse and his piercing eyes and now it seemed like his glory was only a fraction of this great light. Before this light, all eyes were cast down, not because of shame, but because of the radiance and power of its glory. The light that came from this brilliant star felt alive, warm and breathing. Even though it was painfully bright and powerful, it had a familiar elemental feel to it, as though we had known it from a time before which our memories can recall.

As the man lay there, with hand shading his eyes, waves of light began surging over his body. There was such a great power being released from the rays of light that they bleached anything they landed upon. His body was left white, bleached from the light. As he lay there on the ground, tiny little vine-like fibers began to grow up out of the ground and weave together over the contour of his body until he was completely covered in a new, living garment. This new clothing was brilliant. It looked like it was made of natural fibers, almost like long tiny strands of wheat.

The Spirit said, "Your clothes represent your past, your present and your future. They tell where you have been, where you are and where you will be. Inside the walls of Hades, everyone wears the clothes of the past. Like the stones in their walls, their clothes identify where they have been. As you came out of these walls, your clothes are transformed into clothes of the present. They were changed to mark out who you are. But a day is coming, and now is come in which you will be given clothes worthy of where and who you will be forever."

After a time, when his eyes had adjusted a bit more to their new nature, he looked around and noticed that he was on solid ground at the base of the courtyard. A short while longer, and he was able to see the banner and see that there might be an exit as people were going in that direction. He got up and joined the procession and found his way out.

THE STATUED MEN

After this, the Spirit took me back to a place where I could look down onto the wall that surrounded the courtyard. In addition to the dark figures I had seen earlier, there were multitudes of grey, colorless statues of people all over the walls. As I looked closer, I realized they were actually alive. The Spirit began to show me their history. They had not always looked like stone. Many of them had originally been full of life. These were people who had felt a sense of entrapment within the castle, and they longed for answers that could only come through a confrontation with the stone giant. Answers that would only come by being thrown into an unknown place. But because of fear and unbelief, they would never enter the confrontation themselves, but always stayed watching at a safe distance. They were living vicariously, but not truly living. Their only sense of freedom came through watching others experience it. After long periods of time, never moving, they began breathing slower. The longer they stayed, the more grey and cold they became. Barely living, these took on the form of a stone statue.

I thought of the numerous people I knew who had grown so accustomed to going to a church building and sitting in their seat and hearing and seeing the word but never doing the word. I thought of how stuck these people were and how hard it would be to move them into a place of true encounter. They would have to come to a place of such violent desperation if they would ever break off their stone shell and allow themselves to be thrown into the place unknown.

I thought of Matthew 11:12 which says, "From the days of John the Baptist until now the kingdom of heaven suffers violence and violent men take it by force." This is what they must become if they are to come out.

GHOSTS

I also began to see some who looked like ghosts moving from level to level through the walls.

The Spirit said, "These are those who once tasted, but have since forsaken the Word of God and come back up the stairway. They passed twice through the Word of God and thereby gave up the right to their bodies."

I could see that these were people who had become institutionalized. Even though they were at one time given freedom, all that the freedom did for them was make them sure they loved a structure and a cage more than they could ever love a person. To them, all people, including Christ, were subjective and relative variables they could not afford to place their security and trust in. So they returned. But when they did, every step they took back up the stairs caused them to become less and less solid forms or bodies. By the time they reached the top, they lost every part of themselves that could restrict them to a cage. Even though they longed to be caged, their bodies were no longer subject to caging. They were cursed. Learning this, they would now wander through the walls from one level to the next almost always heading to the higher levels, away from the Word of God. Even if they did come to a place within His grasp, His hand would pass right through them. He was unable to grab them, for they had nothing of substance for Him to grab on to.

I thought of the scripture in Hebrews 6:4-10 that says, "For in the case of those who have once been enlightened and have tasted of the heavenly gift and have been made partakers of the Holy Spirit, and have tasted the good word of God and the powers of the age to come, and then have fallen away, it is impossible to renew them again to repentance, since they again crucify to themselves the Son of God and put Him to open shame.   For ground that drinks the rain which often falls on it and brings forth vegetation useful to those for whose sake it is also tilled, receives a blessing from God; but if it yields thorns and thistles, it is worthless and close to being cursed and it ends up being burned. But, beloved, we are convinced of better things concerning you, and things that accompany salvation, though we are speaking in this way. For God is not unjust so as to forget your work and the love which you have shown toward His name, in having ministered and in still ministering to the saints."

I instantly thought of so many of the people in my life who seemed to be ghosts in spirit like this. I became sad and discouraged. I wondered if there was any hope at all for them.

The Spirit reminded me, "With man it is impossible. But with God, all things are possible."

THE STAIRWAY OF SAINTS WHO RETURNED

The stairway that the stone giant stood upon was very hard to see. As I looked more closely I could tell it was unstable—like at any second it might completely evaporate, thereby destroying any chance for the people of the stone castle to be set free. The stairway seemed to be perpetually eroding. It eroded especially fast when the ghost people would come back up it. The stone man Himself never eroded, but the stairway below him did. The more it did, the further the Stone Man would get from the people on the wall level and the harder it was for them to be set free. I assumed the stairway was made of stone because it was strong enough to support the enormous stone man, but I realized that what it was made of was very weak and temporal.

At this moment, a man from the procession suddenly came running back in from outside the gate and he dove into the stairway as if it were a pool of water. As he did this he disappeared into the steps of the stairway. Instantly where he dove, the stairway was changed. It was added to. It became more solid where he dove in. He was like a giant-sized raindrop of cement instantly hardened the stairs which he fell upon. But it was only a few moments after the man had run and dove into the stairway, that the stairway began the process of erosion again. Every so often there would be one or two that would see this great need and run back to strengthen the stairway.

I realized that the stairway was made of the flesh of the men and women of those set free—those who upheld the word of God. Because of this, it was always decaying and eroding. The only way it continued to exist was if the saints of the procession chose to come back into the place from which they had escaped to become the stairway for others. These people were truly sacrificial—true living martyrs.

The Spirit said, "Those to whom great glory is due."

He continued, "It used to take much longer before erosion would set in, but the rate of erosion has increased in your generation."

Panic hit me as I thought of how impossible it seemed for our generation, who seems to know so little of sacrifice, with this increased erosion, to become the stairway that holds the Word of God.

The Spirit said, "Look there."

I looked and saw a few more people turn back and run and dive into the stairway. Then more turned back, then even more. Soon there was a flood of people who had returned to become a living sacrifice unto the Lord. Before long there were so many volunteers that there was a line. There were more than enough people to keep the stairway solidified. They began to dive in systematically—one every two minutes or so.

The Spirit said, "A re-generation of order and strength, faith and selflessness is coming and is already here."

THE SHIFTING WALLS

In another picture, at what seemed like random and unpredictable moments, the castle walls would shift. When they did this, many of the people who were standing next to the walls would fall off their stairways or levels or get smacked by the shifting bricks and mortar. These falls and knocks would often result in broken bones, deep cuts and sometimes even death.

The Spirit said, "This is the nature of religion. As its laws and customs change its new walls cut and kill many of its former servants."

Chapter 6

The Spring of the Gentiles

NEXT I WAS BROUGHT BACK to the front of the castle. My focus was turned to the river which was rapidly flowing from under the drawbridge in two opposite directions around the castle. Even though it was mostly iridescent, the river had an odd, milky color and texture. It looked very deep, as if there were many layers of currents. It was flowing a lot faster under the surface than on top. I thought how river motes were often built to create a barrier of protection around their castle. This is exactly what it seemed to be doing, only this particular river mote seemed to have an even deeper relationship with its stone castle.

The Spirit said, "Sin is lawlessness. And lawlessness, resulting from fear and mistrust, becomes the guardian of man's religion."

The river flowed past a dark black barren tree that had died on the bank of the river on the right side of the castle. On the tree was written 'malice and wickedness.'

The Spirit said, "The name of the mote is 'LUST,' the river is called, 'LAWLESSNESS.' This is the spring of the gentiles."

He continued, "Lust is the mother who cradles her child, Lawlessness."

As I looked at the milky water, The Spirit said, "A river white with the yeast of Herod."

The Spirit seemed to be saying that the primary thing that promotes, protects and even feeds man's religious law is lust and lawlessness. The fact that man was plagued with lust and lawlessness, protected and promoted his need for religious law. Most of the social laws were built primarily to protect man from his own lust and wickedness. The religious laws seemed to be established to provide an illusion of separation, or covering, from one's own lust and wickedness even though it often accomplished the complete opposite.

The Spirit said, "From the time of the fall of Adam, lust has been the inheritance of man. And since then, man has built many structures within and upon its void. If they are to escape the fate of the castle, they must come out from its walls and come out from its island altogether."

All of these laws which made up the multi-layered castle had only been birthed out of a reaction to the negative circumstances of the island. The people that established and built up all these walls could not see that the problem was the island of isolation itself. Even though they had made many nice and sturdy structures, ideologies and religions, they had built their structures on the wrong foundation to begin with—on an island of isolation and insecurity. And even though one might be able to argue that many of the island's laws were based on good motives, nothing was yet offered that could take the people off the island. For this reason, I could see why God might hate these laws and structures that give a false security and a false sense of innocence. They all seemed to fail to offer a way off of the island itself.

CARELESS MEN

Next I saw two men who had made it over the bridge. They had been freed from the castle to follow the procession, but they became distracted by the beauty and mystery of the river. They had grown up their whole lives inside the castle, but had never known the source of their water supply and that the river flowed so close to where they had lived all their lives. They made their way down the steep bank and stood next to it, talking quite frivolously without a care or concern in the world.

Then to my surprise, many of these people began jumping into the river. There were others who were falling in as a result of being pushed, or being careless and slipping, but the majority of the people who came to the river were choosing willfully to jump in. They thought floating in this river looked more appealing than marching in a procession. This was startling to me. I sensed the Spirit surge within me with emotion. I was torn between crying and screaming. I began to mourn the death and destiny of these men.

As I wept, I heard the Spirit say, "True grief belongs to me."

It was the Spirit who was grieving in me at the sight of the people in this river.

The Spirit said, "Salvation is not of outward works, but of inward works. Inward is in the form of choice. If one refuses to choose the grace of God, limited grace can be received. If one chooses to accept the grace of God, infinite grace can be given. It is a working of the will. Choice is in the realm of the will. Too many people mistake the scriptures to mean that it is not of works at all in the sense that there is no change needed; they make this doctrine into an excuse for self and sin. Do not mistake choice for works. But don't mistake choice for non-works either. Choice is in a different category from outer works. Outer works involve the movement of flesh. Inward choice involves the movement of will. I desire choice. Works are merely the blessing or the curse of free choice."

I realized by this that there is not a thing we can do in the flesh as a work to earn the free gift of light and life. Our earthly bodies can lay comatose, without movement for 100 years and accomplish the same grace and favor as one who has used those thousand years to build an empire. No carnal work can merit the free gift of God's grace. But grace is designed to place enormous demands on the souls and spirits of all who choose it. The result is an epic journey riddled with choice after choice each with its own temptations, opportunities, traumas, deficits or rewards. Choice is the journey we are on. Our choices are what prove us. A choice is an inward decision and if truly made, it will manifest in an outward action.

THREE MEN WHO CHOSE THE RIVER

Many people were choosing to go to the river willfully. At this point, the Spirit brought me before three of them. He allowed me to see right into their minds and hearts. It was as if their eyes were a window into their souls.

THE FIRST TO COME TO THE RIVER

I looked into the eyes of the first one and saw doubt. When he had been in the castle, he was often disgusted by the senseless content of the people who were born and raised on one level and who now seemed to blindly accept, support and advocate the laws of their floor without respect or concern for any laws that might exist beyond their own. They were content to stay there, living according to the law of their religious level without any regard to the rest of mankind. They were never able or willing to see the stairways—much less the open sky. For him on the other hand, the open skies had become his only real enjoyment in life and he despised his inherited hunchback because it made it all the harder for him to see that which he had come to so enjoy.

To him, the people who were content looking down upon their level seemed like empty shells. He began to have major doubts about the purpose of the walls and floor. But when he was asked, it was hard for him to offer any objective reason for his doubt. He had only the power and light to see that the bricks on that floor did not contain the answer. Because of this, he often sat alone in silence and frustration. His frustration drove him to discover stairway after stairway and his disgust for senseless content often brought him down in humility instead of up in pride. So after he had survived traveling from level to level of man's law, he eventually found himself at the stone giant. As desperate and frustrated as he had become, he wasn't afraid to be broken and he didn't hesitate to be thrown into a place unknown.

When this man first saw the white horse, he was overwhelmed with joy as he began to believe that he had finally found what he had been looking for. But as he persevered and persisted in the gate, and then marched in the procession across the bridge, his eyes were eventually turned to the people around him, many of whom, as they fixed on the Horse, reminded him of those within the castle who possessed that senseless content of which he had come to so hate. They were so eager to believe and follow the status quo, without reason or question. It was not long before his hatred and speculation became a lens by which he saw everything.

As he looked upon the white horse—now filtered through doubt and skepticism, he found it hard to believe that the white horse cared about his well being. He began to doubt the horse even knew where he was going. He began to think of the procession as just a different type of religious level. Within minutes, the horse was out of direct sight and he began to wonder if all along the horse were merely a figment level for desperate imaginations—one with a horse that is nice to follow.

As this man saw the river, he saw an escape, a place to take a break, a place of independence where he was free from all association. To him this meant freedom from having to trust or invest in something he couldn't control, and it also meant freedom from his own hatred and resentment towards those who were willing to trust and invest in what they couldn't control.

The Spirit said, "Faith relinquishes its control to another. Your faith in Me is subject to your trust in My love for you. When sons and daughters do not trust in the present goodness of their Father, they will not relinquish their present control to Him."

This man did not trust in God's goodness. He doubted God's love for him. He felt more at home with the water than with the procession. The water as a substance was always moving and able to bend around the rocks and structures of man. Like him, it was also unset in its purpose, it was easily moved in contrast to the rocks of the castle. But it was not directed by anyone, unlike the procession. For this reason, because he was unset, and because he was familiar with adjusting and bending around rocks, the river was the most familiar thing he had come to see. He saw it as a place of his own identity—his home. There, he could gather his thoughts and take a break.

The Spirit said, "His name is 'Doubt.'"

THE SECOND TO COME TO THE RIVER

Then as I looked into the eyes of the second man; I saw great apathy—like numbness. His eyes and his eyebrows were flat, glazed over and unaffected. While in the castle, he had begun to believe in the people and the law of his birth floor. He invested his heart and soul into these people. But then time after time, people failed him. Some left that floor and some stayed, but they didn't produce the life their ideals suggested—what they taught others to keep.

He had invested himself; he was a passionate one, his hope easily roused. He searched for love, hope, and life in every place he went. Eventually he saw a stairway and moved to the next level. His hopeful ambition often led him upward, where he would get his hopes up and be let down. Eventually he ended up at the bottom after passing through many different levels. He blamed himself for every invested hope which failed. These failures weighed down on him and every time he left more apathetic, depressed and hopeless.

He began to develop a hatred of man; which especially included himself. He despised man's need. For it was the only reason that he himself had been so ambitious in the first place. Man's need was weakness. Because of his hatred for man's weakness, every time he failed, he hated himself more and more. The only way for him to be strong was to stop trying all together.

Looking desensitized and brainwashed, he now showed little facial expression regardless of what he looked at. When he had first seen the white horse, his heart sparked a flame and his hope was aroused. But when he was reminded of the danger of investment and his own tendency towards failure, it didn't take long to dismantle his hope and get himself to view the white horse with the same indifference with which he had come to view all other things. It was actually a fear of investment and failure mixed with a hatred of self that led him. Investment itself now became the enemy, without regard to the object or value of investment.

The Spirit said, "There are many of these: depressed, suicidal. Hope must be restored for depression to be cured."

I thought of the great number of people within my generation who have an issue with depression. I myself used to be one of them. The only reason I had personally gotten over my own depression was because I realized that depression was a form of self centeredness and that it was a choice. I didn't have to be depressed if I didn't want to. So it became an issue of my will. After this realization, it seemed silly for me to make the choice to mope around being depressed and self centered. So depression quickly seemed to move out of my lifestyle. Because of this, I told many people that the best cure for depression was to get over self.

The Spirit said, "Yes. Self is what sucks you in, but hope is what sends you out."

He continued, "Many of those who are most depressed in your generation are those who I have called to become prophets of My Kingdom. This is why they are depressed; I have put it in them to know My hope, so they might foretell the future accurately. But when these are suffered to live without hope and remain without their gift being activated, they despair for they cannot see the good in their future and they don't know how they ever will. Death often comes to offer these a short cut, but it is not a shortcut to life, but to destruction."

As He said this, I looked again at this second man who went to the river. As he watched the people within the procession ascend the heights and glory that God had called them to, all he was thinking about was the numerous reasons why his own limitations and disabilities would prevent him from doing the same. He couldn't seem to see that God's favor and grace for him far exceeded any disability or limitation that he had.

The Spirit said, "If he only knew Me and the hope of My calling, I would fulfill his calling. Hope does not disappoint. Hope not only has the power to bring you out of despair, but to bring you into glory."

The Spirit seemed to be saying that the cure for depression was the hope of God. But for people to experience the hope of God, they would first have to overcome their own fear of disappointment. They would also need to be shown their purpose and their future through the eyes of God.

The second man could not seem to overcome his own fear of disappointment. He was nowhere near seeing himself through the eyes of God. To him, the river seemed like an escape from investment—a place free from hope and free from expectation. His vigor and his zeal in the former years would have made him a hard worker no matter what he chose, but now, with motive crushed, laziness and leisure became the central goal of his life. To him, the river was the most comfortable place to be. Like him, its water chose the path of least resistance, the place of greatest convenience. The procession seemed too great an investment. Time and time again, I saw thoughts of excitement and hope flair up about the horse and its procession, only to be crushed by the memories of past failures.

The Spirit said, "'Apathy' is his name."

THE THIRD TO COME TO THE RIVER

As I was brought before the third man, I saw tremendous fear and self-centeredness. This man looked upon the stone castle with great frustration and discontent, like a child might look at an abusive and violent father. In the back of his head was the idea that all people only had the ability to take and not give. With his guard up, he fended and fought for everything that he could possibly lay claim to. He justified his own selfishness by reasoning it was merely his reaction to those who had taken from him without giving back. In his spirit, he had become a consumer, always insisting on getting the better deal no matter to whom or to where he went. Giving was a foreign idea to him. In the back of his head, he would tell himself that if he didn't fend for himself, no one else would and he would end up stripped naked of all that was his. Day after day, he constantly lived under this fear.

Any time a new person would reach out to him, he would immediately assume that they had only come to him to take advantage of him. On his own birth floor, he had been severely neglected and abused. Out of desperation for survival, he managed to find a stairway out. At first when he came to the next floor, he began to allow himself to trust again, even to give again. Yet he would always seem to find a reason to fear that those around him were only out to use or abuse him. Because of this he began to see all authority as the enemy and as the slave drivers of all. On each level he trained himself to identify those in authority and to imagine every kind of abuse their power might allow them to participate in. He projected his own heart and motive on others and assumed that it was true.

He was utterly alone, yet he longed for a companion who was suitable for him, but because of his selfishness and his suspicion, few, if any, took the time to invest in him. Fear produced a growing shame, rage and self-centeredness in him.

He moved from level to level partially to escape relationships that weren't meeting his desires and partially to search for ones that could. Before long, he happened to end up at the lowest level. It was only by accident that he ended up in the grasp of the stone man. The stone man to him was the most horrifying thing he had ever seen.

When he first came to the white horse, he saw the white horse as one who would finally be able to fulfill all of his desires. He tried time and time again to get the white horse to suit his will, yet he never could. It wasn't long before he began to reason that this horse didn't care about his desires. The horse seemed to have a different Owner and he was only willing to obey Him.

Now in second consideration, he became angry with himself for forgetting that the white horse was also one who seemed to have authority, and for this reason he was to be feared and looked upon with suspicion. He soon found ways to suspect the worst and told himself the very one who freed him from the castle only did so to take a worse kind of advantage of him. He determined he would not be mastered by anyone. His fear made him despise and hate anything that could gain entrance into his heart. His hate became his shield to guard himself from those who would love him.

As I looked at this man, I thought of all the people I knew who out of fear, independence or rebellion, had forsaken those that love them the most—those that they are meant to be with.

To this man the river seemed like an endless source—a place where he could take without ever needing to give back, a place where he would always get the better deal. He saw the river as a thing that he could always manipulate to serve his own purposes. It was beautiful, drinkable, it was below him. There was no authority in that place. There was no fear of abuse. It was dead.

The Spirit said, "This is the hardest of the three kinds of men."

It seemed like almost everyone who was once freed from the castle but then turned aside to the river, fit into one or a combination of these three types of men. And the river wasted no time, always seducing, always luring, tempting its victims deeper and deeper until they were too deep to fight the current and they were swept away.

Then I saw there was one other type of person who came to the river banks. This person's clothes were still dirty. They had somehow escaped from the castle, but without being broken by the stone giant or cleansed by the light.

The Spirit said, "Counterfeits."

At first glance, I hardly noticed the ones with dirty clothes. But as I looked closer at those emerging from the gate, I realized it was closer to a quarter of them who were dressed this way. As soon as these unclean ones had a chance to break ranks from the procession they would rush immediately to the banks of the river of lust. Yet they rarely ever got their feet wet. They loved the entertainment of lust and wickedness but they also hated the thought of being under the control of anything besides themselves. Thus they never went in past their ankles.

The Spirit said, "Gossips, slanderers, hypocrites, procrastinators and liars. They claim to be delivered from Death, yet they still love his entertainment."

He continued, "These are they of whom Isaiah prophesied when he said, 'We'll eat our own bread, and wear our own clothes: only let us be called by Thy name, take away our reproach.'"

It seemed to me that the three men who were named, "Doubt," "Apathy," and "Fear" might represent the opposite of the abiding faith, hope and love which will transcend the ages of man. 1 Corinthians 13:13 says "But now faith, hope, love, abide these three; but the greatest of these is love."

In all of this, those who kept their focus on the white horse who led the procession kept marching on.

Chapter 7

The Mote of Mammon

I LOOKED EVEN CLOSER at the mote. I noticed the banks of the river mote were lined with money.

The Spirit said, "The love of money is the root of all kinds of evil. There are many who have bowed their knee to mammon."

As He said this, I was stricken by all the times I had questioned the promises of God on account of money and all the times I let money dictate Gods ability and my own limitations. I thought of how easy it is in the church as a paid minister to bow the knee to mammon. I wondered how much I might do differently if I didn't have to create a paycheck out of ministry each month. I thought about how so much of the western church has become such a business. I wondered how many decisions were being made in the church in order to maintain income or worldly success instead of out of a pure faith and devotion to God.

Then I thought, "Yes, but money in itself isn't bad, it's the love of money that is the root of all kinds of evil."

The Spirit said, "Yes, the love of money. But it is also the worship of money that I despise. You have said that you will always worship what you fear the most. This is true. It is also true that whatever a man places his security in will become the thing he serves. If you seek security in money, money will become your master."

He continued. "What you seek to possess will often become the thing that ends up possessing you. So many have become possessed by the riches of this world. Mammon is not merely a name for money, it's the name of a demon. His yoke is not easy, his burden is not light and just like all devils, he does not possess the power or the will to give life, but only to take it. He shares the same fate as all the enemies of God's image and likeness. His fate is destruction."

I thought of Luke 16:13, which says, "No servant can serve two masters; for either he will hate the one and love the other, or else he will be devoted to one and despise the other. You cannot serve both God and mammon."

After a moment, I returned to the thought I had earlier, "Yes but money in itself isn't bad, is it? We need it to survive, don't we?"

The Spirit answered again, "So many of you think and pray to Me about money as if I had any of it, as if money originated with Us. Money has no place in heaven just as want has no place in heaven, and just as debt has no place in heaven. Yes I can create it if I choose to. I can and do answer many cries for provision in every way. Yet I tell you that while money is a major force within the world as you know it, the world as you know it is temporal, and so are its powers. And while I do provide temporal solutions for temporal problems, I tell you that I have set a time in which all temporal things will be consumed by that which is eternal, and all mortal things by that which is immortal."

I thought of the passage that says, "Now I say this, brethren, that flesh and blood cannot inherit the kingdom of God; nor does the perishable inherit the imperishable. Behold, I tell you a mystery; we will not all sleep, but we will all be changed, in a moment, in the twinkling of an eye, at the last trumpet; for the trumpet will sound, and the dead will be raised imperishable, and we will be changed. For this perishable must put on the imperishable, and this mortal must put on immortality. But when this perishable will have put on the imperishable, and this mortal will have put on immortality, then will come about the saying that is written, "Death is swallowed up in victory. O death, where is your victory? O death, where is your sting?" The sting of death is sin, and the power of sin is the law; but thanks be to God, who gives us the victory through our Lord Jesus Christ." - 1 Corinthians 15:50-57

THE ECONOMY OF HEAVEN

I returned to the idea that there is no money in heaven. I wondered at how different heaven must be from earth. I wondered how it could be possible to have a society that did not use money.

The Holy Spirit spoke again, "The mote you see is the void created by independence. Independence is the void in which lust is conceived. Lust is the inventor of money. You were never meant to be alone. You were never meant to be independent from Me. Because of the lie of independence, all kinds of vile inventions have come to be. Yet there is no independence in heaven, and therefore, no need for money. In heaven, all things are one."

I thought of the passage that says, "Owe nothing to anyone except to love one another; for he who loves his neighbor has fulfilled the law." - Romans 13:8

I also thought of the scripture that says, "Freely you received, freely give." - Matthew 10:8

After a moment He continued, "There is no need to claim ownership in heaven because all ownership has already been claimed. There is no need to define worth in heaven because all worth has already been defined. There is no need to trade in heaven because all things have already been traded. All things belong to Him to whom we all belong."

He continued, "This will be hard for many of you to understand but you should know that money is not part of the economy of heaven. You invented money. You invented debt. Not Us. You created money as a means to keep track of the deception of independent ownership. Why would We need money to keep track of what We give freely? "Why would We want more than We already have? Do you think We lust like you do to gain more? Why would We keep track of the resources We give when Our resources are infinite? Why would We hold a debt against Our own offspring? The Kingdom belongs to you already. Are you not all equal members of My image and likeness? Are you not all heirs to all that is Mine?"

I thought of the account of the early church in the book of Acts and how they seemed to be living by these values. It says, "And the congregation of those who believed were of one heart and soul; and not one of them claimed that anything belonging to him was his own, but all things were common property to them." - Acts 4:32

I also thought of the passage that says, "Look at the birds of the air, that they do not sow, nor reap nor gather into barns, and yet your heavenly Father feeds them. Are you not worth much more than they?" -Matthew 6:26

The Spirit spoke again, this time more softly, "It's not only so with heaven."

He paused for a moment. Then continued, "The earth and its riches also belong to all of you already. I gave it to you as an inheritance, but you fight over it as if you all came from different families. It is only because you have believed the lie of independence that you claim ownership over anything. This lie came in the garden when the serpent caused Eve to question her dependence on God. The serpent told her, 'God knows that in the day you eat from it your eyes will be opened, and you will be like God...' (Genesis 3:5) She already was like Him. She was made in His image and likeness. Yet in the serpent's subtle accusation, the lie of isolation was established. Independence was born, and from that day the false sense of isolation and independence has been the cause of every evil thing upon the earth. Isolation and independence is the root of all sin. It is the root of all lies, all false religion and the origin of all lust and wickedness.

My mind was racing to try to understand all the implications of what was just said. Before I had a chance to conclude anything, the Spirit spoke again, "Babylon was the origin of your monetary debt system and the serpent in the garden was the origin of Babylon's inception."

I wanted to protest a little bit. I thought, "But there are many things which we possess that we created and worked for and earned. Wouldn't it be right for those things to be our own?

He answered, "Yes, but consider those things."

It was only a few futile moments of consideration before I concluded that He had already given me all the things I truly needed. And the things I worked for and earned or created myself were either worthless things I would be embarrassed to admit or worthy things He put in me to do. I had to admit I had gone after these things in the first place because He gave me an able mind, body and will to do so. He gave me the very life I used to go after those things. I imagined it would be like an oven that starts arguing with the baker over who owns the food being baked in the oven. What I produced with the abilities he gave me was not mine, but His.

I thought of the scripture, "I am the vine, you are the branches; he who abides in Me and I in him, he bears much fruit, for apart from Me you can do nothing." - John 15:5

He said, "It is true. All the fruit of your labor belongs to the One who planted you and gave you life. Nevertheless, I tell you that if you will not claim anything as your own, then I will give you the right to share in the ownership of everything."

THE USE OF MONEY

I looked at the banks of the river filled with all kinds of money bills. I said, "Well then, do we just let people take everything from us? What about my family? How will I provide for them? We will just get taken advantage of. We can't just forsake money altogether and let random people move into our house, can we? My family would be miserable.

He answered, "Yes, you are called to care for those in need to the extent that you are able, but be wise as serpents and innocent as doves. Use your material wealth to buy for yourselves the true riches in heaven. If you have a place, use it to take in orphans and widows in the time of their distress. What you possess, employ it to love. Use it in the way you would think I would use it. Know that I want you to prosper and I want you to enjoy life! Take care of yourselves, and care for those around you. There is always enough to love. You will always have enough if you will love."

I thought of the passage that says, "Make friends for yourselves by means of the wealth of unrighteousness, so that when it fails, they will receive you into the eternal dwellings. He who is faithful in a very little thing is faithful also in much; and he who is unrighteous in a very little thing is unrighteous also in much. Therefore if you have not been faithful in the use of unrighteous wealth, who will entrust the true riches to you? - Luke 16:9-11

He continued, "Money is not meant to be served but it can and should be used to serve. This is the difference. Mammon convinces humanity to keep records, debts, and accounts of money. Love convinces humanity to keep no record, to forgive all debt and to take not into account any wrong suffered."

After a pause, He continued, "You can do this without being taken advantage of and your family would actually love it if you would lead them to love."

I paused to think about what He was saying. He wasn't saying to quit my job, to let people take my belongings, and sit around doing nothing. He was saying the opposite of that. He was saying to work hard so that I was in the position to love.

"Yes," He said, "You were created to create. The fruit of your labor should not only be able to provide for you, it should be able to provide for others as well. If your creativity is not providing for you, then it is motivation for you to do it better. That is why I don't make it easier. The pressure makes you perfect your gift. The pressure refines your produce. Everyone is working in heaven. Everyone enjoys a job and they are excellent at their job. As it is in heaven, so shall it be upon the earth. If God entrusts you with something, it is to see what will happen to that thing under your care. For this purpose you are called to steward what the Father has given to you."

I began to think of all the things God had entrusted to me. My family was the first thought that came to mind. Then I thought about the ministries I was involved in and then my talents, gifts and skills.

The Spirit said, "Protect the family God has entrusted to you. Provide for them. Prosper them. And teach them to protect, provide for and prosper others. Protect the ministry God has entrusted to you. Provide for it. Prosper it. And cause it to protect, provide for and prosper others. Protect the talents, gifts and skills God has entrusted to you. Provide for them. Prosper them. And cause them to protect, provide for and prosper others. Protect the property God entrusts to you. Provide for it. Prosper it. And use it for the sake of love. Use these things to further the administration of grace."

Chapter 8

The Seeds of Life

MY ATTENTION TURNED AGAIN to the procession. The Holy Spirit was highlighting everyone's clothing. Each person was wearing the clothing that had grown onto them in the light of Abraham after they had been crushed by the stone giant. The Spirit allowed me to see the clothing up close. It was made of a beautiful, thin, earthy material, almost like lots of little golden blades of grass, or perhaps more like thin alfalfa sprouts all woven together to make a beautiful pattern. I was shown that over the course of many hours, these garments were slowly but steadily growing. And over the course of a day, the garments would produce many pieces of fruit. It was small fruit, like mini cherries or mini olives. These were living, fruit-bearing garments.

THE TRUE VINE & ITS FRUIT

As I watched these beautiful vines cover the people as clothing and I saw the fruit growing, I thought about how every piece of fruit contained a seed.

The Spirit said, "Yes, almost every seed is delivered in the package of fruit. Without the fruit, the seeds are unprotected. It is the same with the seeds God has placed in you."

As He spoke I was picturing God take an idea and package it in the form of a seed. Then I pictured Him putting His idea in someone's mind. I understood that He was saying that without the fruit of the Spirit, the seeds of the Spirit—the ideas of God, are not in the right environment to produce life. Instead, they are in danger of being stolen, consumed or destroyed.

The Spirit said, Every fruit attached to the Vine will reproduce it's seed."

As I looked at these garments, I thought about how every seed bearing fruit had vine growing potential. I became fascinated with watching the growth of the Vine. The sight of it was beautiful.

The Spirit said, "The true vine."

I remembered the passage in John 15 where Jesus says, "I am the true vine, and my Father is the vinedresser. Every branch in me that does not bear fruit he takes away, and every branch that does bear fruit he prunes, that it may bear more fruit. Already you are clean because of the word that I have spoken to you. Abide in me, and I in you. As the branch cannot bear fruit by itself, unless it abides in the vine, neither can you, unless you abide in me. I am the vine; you are the branches. Whoever abides in me and I in him will bear much fruit, for apart from me you can do nothing. If anyone does not abide in me he is thrown away like a branch and withers; and the branches are gathered, thrown into the fire, and burned. If you abide in me, and my words abide in you, ask whatever you wish, and it will be done for you. By this my Father is glorified, that you bear much fruit and so prove to be my disciples. - John 15:1-8

I became curious about what the people in the procession would do with the fruit. I was able to watch them as time sped over a few days. Every evening and every morning the people would have to pick the fruit off their garments so they didn't get weighed down by it. Every morning and every evening I saw people taking their fruit in one of two directions. Some would take their fruit and plant it on the grassy hills along side of the procession and others would take their fruit to the river banks to trade them or gamble them. Everyone seemed to end up casting their fruits where their attention was most aimed.

I noticed one person who took their fruit and exchanged it at a little stone room that had been built right next to the river. It was a type of bank with bank tellers and all. As the man presented his fruits to the teller, they would be weighed and a monetary value was placed on the fruit, then the teller would report the weight to one of the bank owners and the owner would approve or disapprove the exchange. If the exchange was approved, the banker would take the fruit and exchange it for money notes. In this particular instance, the man took the money and began to gamble it at the river. I could see that to the bank owners, the money itself was useless. It was not the money, but the fruit of peoples' lives that they fed off of.

At the end of each day, the bank owners would divide up the fruit and give the tellers a small percentage as commission for their work, keeping a huge percentage for themselves. The portion the bankers kept was always way too large for them to be able to eat themselves so their stockpiles just kept getting larger and larger, and much of it had become rotten. I saw the bankers throwing stacks of bills into the river and although I did not know the reason, this explained why the banks of the mote were littered with bills. The money lining the banks of the river represented fruit sown in the wrong place–life that produced rotten fruit.

The Spirit said, "These are seeds of time sown on infertile soil and the fruit of works sown in lust."

As He said this I began thinking that the fruit from these garments might represent our works, ideas, energy and time.

LIFE IS IN THE SEED

I looked again at the people in the procession that sowed their seed on the hills next to the trail. As I turned to them I had a vision. In the vision I saw a man sow a seed, and as time went by the seed began to grow and turned into a tree. Over more time this tree began producing fruit and dropping it. Time sped up again, and an entire forest had sprung up from the regeneration of that first tree. Then time sped up again, and I received a higher view. I saw multitudes of seeds, produced from the forest, spreading out and producing trees across the entire continent.

"Of the increase of the forest of My Kingdom there shall be no end," the Spirit said, partially quoting Isaiah 9:7.

The Spirit continued, "Forests that grow to cover entire regions and nations start with one seed. So as with all life, it also is with all faith and every idea. The largest of all the living things comes from that which is small. The mightiest trees first begin with a tiny seed. The largest animals first begin with a tiny seed. No matter how big or small, life begins with a small seed. This is the way of all the living."

As He was speaking, I thought of the parable of the mustard seed, "Jesus presented another parable to them, saying, 'The kingdom of heaven is like a mustard seed, which a man took and sowed in his field; and this is smaller than all other seeds, but when it is full grown, it is larger than the garden plants and becomes a tree, so that the birds of the air come and nest in its branches.'"

He continued, "This is how it is with every thought that God places in your mind. The Gospel itself is only first delivered as a message, a seed. If it lands on good soil, it can grow into a mighty tree, even strong enough to carry the soil it lies within."

I thought, "How does a tree carry the soil it lies within?"

He answered, "The way you identify a land is based on the types of seeds it accepts: a forest, a prairie, or a desert. These are all names describing lands that accept different seeds. So the identity of the soil is dependent on what seeds it grows. It is the same with you."

I thought of Jesus' parable of the sower. "And He spoke many things to them in parables, saying, 'Behold, the sower went out to sow; and as he sowed, some seeds fell beside the road, and the birds came and ate them up. Others fell on the rocky places, where they did not have much soil; and immediately they sprang up, because they had no depth of soil. But when the sun had risen, they were scorched; and because they had no root, they withered away. Others fell among the thorns, and the thorns came up and choked them out. And others fell on the good soil and yielded a crop, some a hundredfold, some sixty, and some thirty. He who has ears, let him hear.' Hear then the parable of the sower. When anyone hears the word of the kingdom and does not understand it, the evil one comes and snatches away what has been sown in his heart. This is the one on whom seed was sown beside the road. The one on whom seed was sown on the rocky places, this is the man who hears the word and immediately receives it with joy; yet he has no firm root in himself, but is only temporary, and when affliction or persecution arises because of the word, immediately he falls away. And the one on whom seed was sown among the thorns, this is the man who hears the word, and the worry of the world and the deceitfulness of wealth choke the word, and it becomes unfruitful. And the one on whom seed was sown on the good soil, this is the man who hears the word and understands it; who indeed bears fruit and brings forth, some a hundredfold, some sixty, and some thirty." - Matthew 13:3-9, 18-23

After I had read and thought about the parable of the sower, the Spirit said, "God's seeds are full of life's potential. It is not a question of the seed being good, but the environment the seed is placed in that determines how much of its potential it will reach. A good seed can lie dormant, without life for many years, but when the right environment presents itself, all of a sudden, life comes forth. The soil only possesses life if it contains a seed. The expressions of life you possess are only manifestations of the seeds you have nurtured. The life is in the seed. The soil only determines when, where and if each seed will produce."

He continued, "It is the same with the gifts your Father gives to you. The gifts the Father gives, He gives to you in seed form. Your life was first a seed, your family was first a seed, and your ministry was first a seed. Likewise, your career, your relationships and your property, even your dreams and desires are all first given as seeds. God's gifts are His seeds."

He continued in strong tone, "Every single seed possesses the fullness of the potential of the life of its species. Every seed has the power to perfectly remember its past and perfectly predict its future. Life's future is conceived in the seeds from its past. Without your seed, your future cannot be conceived. Once the seed ceases to exist, the life form also will cease to exist. So long as the seed exists, there is yet still hope for that life form to exist."

I began thinking of all the things I had been given from God.

The Spirit continued, "Each seed He gives, He gives to prove your heart. How His seeds grow in you shows how your heart has grown in Him. He gives you seeds to show you the soil of your heart, and the water, the light and the elements you allow in."

He continued, "His seed, sown in you, reveals who He thinks you are. How you grow His seed reveals who you think you are."

I wondered if the scripture said anything else about seeds. I found this passage, "...Love one another earnestly from a pure heart, since you have been born again, not of perishable seed but of imperishable, through the living and abiding word of God; for all flesh is like grass and all its glory like the flower of grass. The grass withers, and the flower falls, but the word of the Lord remains forever. And this word is the good news that was preached to you." - 1 Peter 1:22-25

I found another passage, "The apostles said to the Lord, 'Increase our faith!' And the Lord said, 'If you had faith like a grain of mustard seed, you could say to this mulberry tree, 'Be uprooted and planted in the sea,' and it would obey you.'" - Luke 17:5 -

"Wow." I thought to myself, "The gospel is referred to as a seed and faith is also referred to as a seed."

The Spirit said, "My Word is My seed in you, your faith is your seed in Me."

GOD'S SEED IS OMNIPRESENT

Then the Spirit said, "I want to show you the life that is in the seed."

As He said this, a piece of fruit appeared before me. The fruit was cut in half so you could see the seed inside. Then the seed opened and I saw what looked like an entire universe inside. I was seeing the DNA of the seed. It was vast. To me, it seemed more infinite than any universe I could ever imagine.

"You don't understand God's size." The Spirit said. "You think God is so big that He is everywhere, like a big floating cloud that stretches from universe to universe. And in a way that is true; He is almighty and all-powerful, He does manifest Himself as a cloud or as fire or as wind or as water or however He wants. But it is not the way you think. God is everywhere because His seed is everywhere. God is a being in heaven, but He is also His seed in you. All of His fullness is contained in every molecule of His creation. All of creation declares His glory. His presence is wherever the seed of His Word has been sown."

I thought to myself, "That's not true. He is everywhere, regardless of if His Word is being sown."

The Spirit said, "You don't understand. His Word is everywhere because His Word is everything. And He is before all things, and in Him all things hold together. He is the image of the invisible God, the firstborn of all creation. For by Him all things were created, in heaven and on earth, visible and invisible, whether thrones or dominions or rulers or authorities—all things were created through Him and for Him. This is what Christ came to reveal to you." He said this, partially quoting Colossians 1:15-17.

He continued, "He is more like the tiny atoms that hold everything together than like some giant man who's body is bigger than the universe. He is Spirit and He is beyond your measurements of time or space. He is the breath that holds all substance together. He holds the universe in His hand and by His Word."

He continued, "He is also more like Adam than you could now understand. And without the first Adam none others could exist."

I paused to think about what He was saying. What is God like? If He is Spirit, how could we be made in His likeness and image?

The Spirit replied, "His Spirit has form. You are not wrong in your thinking. You were created in His image and in His likeness. You are spirit, but you are also flesh. He is Spirit, and He is also flesh. His Word was sent to reveal to you who you are: your likeness to Him. If His Word abides in you then indeed, you will grow like Him. His seed produces His likeness."

I thought of the passage in Genesis 1:11-12, "Then God said, 'Let the earth sprout vegetation, plants yielding seed, *and* fruit trees on the earth bearing fruit after their kind with seed in them;' and it was so. The earth brought forth vegetation, plants yielding seed after their kind, and trees bearing fruit with seed in them, after their kind; and God saw that it was good."

I thought about how each seed only has the power to produce the image and likeness of the thing that it came from. Orange seeds only produce orange trees and cherry seeds only produce cherry trees. I thought about how we are God's seed, and it is in our nature to grow into His likeness.

A passage came to mind, "For those whom he foreknew he also predestined to be conformed to the image of his Son, in order that he might be the firstborn among many brothers." - Romans 8:29

BEWARE WHICH SEEDS YOU NURTURE

The Spirit continued, "But beware, for your enemy also seeks the soil of your heart. Be sure he does not find a place to sow his seeds. If allowed to grow, they will grow into loss, death and destruction."

As He said this, I kept picturing the parable of the tares among wheat. "Jesus presented another parable to them saying, 'The kingdom of heaven may be compared to a man who sowed good seed in his field. But while his men were sleeping, his enemy came and sowed tares among the wheat, and went away. But when the wheat sprouted and bore grain, then the tares became evident also. The slaves of the landowner came and said to him, 'Sir, did you not sow good seed in your field? How then does it have tares?' And he said to them, 'An enemy has done this!' The slaves said to him, 'Do you want us, then, to go and gather them up?' But he said, 'No; for while you are gathering up the tares, you may uproot the wheat with them. Allow both to grow together until the harvest; and in the time of the harvest I will say to the reapers, 'First gather up the tares and bind them in bundles to burn them up; but gather the wheat into my barn.''" - Matthew 13: 24-30

I also thought of the passage that says, "Now He who supplies seed to the sower and bread for food will supply and multiply your seed for sowing and increase the harvest of your righteousness." - 2 Corinthians 9:10

MIDDLE AGED MAN

After a pause, the Spirit spoke again, "The ideas you hold about Me and about yourself are mixed at a middle age." As He said this I knew He was not just saying this to me as an individual, but He was referring to us as the entire human race.

He continued, "Your thoughts are at a crucial turning. So are your governments. Evolution is taking place but the outcome is not final. If the Light remains hidden, you will soon suffer great loss."

Again, I felt He was emphasizing the human race as a whole. As I considered His words I became gripped with fear. I imagined a nuclear world war or any number of cataclysms taking place that would wipe out the human race. "Are we all just going to die from some horrible thing?" I began to wonder.

The Spirit answered, "It is appointed for man to die once and after that to face judgment. Yet, imperishable seeds planted bear imperishable fruit. And already he who reaps is receiving his wages and is gathering up his fruit for life eternal so that he who sows and he who reaps may rejoice together." He said this, partially quoting Hebrews 9:27 and John 4:36.

Chapter 9

The Procession

IN THE NEXT PICTURE, it had suddenly become much darker on the path. It was night time. No one in the procession was able to see where they were going. The white horse had gotten very far ahead of the procession and he was hard to see now.

THE THREE LAMPHOLDERS

Then a man emerged from the procession holding a tall black lamp post in his right hand that was about twelve feet tall with a very bright light at the top. This man seemed to be different, he was separate from all the other people. The man himself was larger than the rest of the people, he stood about 8 feet tall and he looked very strong and handsome. The light at the top of the lamp post came from a type of candle with flame, but it was brighter than any candle I had ever seen. It lit a radius of about 100 feet all around him. He went and stood about 15 feet off to the side of the procession. There he held his lamp post so that it brought the maximum amount of light down upon the procession in the direction from where he had come so that they could see how to get to him. This was very helpful for the people who were behind him in the procession. In his left hand he had a shield. His shield was made of some kind of metal covered with red leather and a bronze frame around it. In the center was a carving of the white horse.

Once he had pointed his light back down upon the path for all the people behind him, I noticed that he then planted and drove the bottom end of the lamp post deep into the ground so that the lamp would be hard to move. As he did this, I had the sense he was forfeiting his ability to go any further for the sake of providing a light to those who were behind him. This man was glorious in a unique way; he was both sacrificial and noble.

As soon as this man had planted his lamp post, a multitude of people gathered around him. It was like a room being filled from wall to wall with people. Light was the most valuable commodity of this hour. There was standing room only. No one wanted to venture out past where the lamp holder was because it was dark and yet more and more people kept flooding in. At first this lamp holder's light was a relief. But within moments, there was not enough room for all of the people to fit. The ones who couldn't find a place in his light were forced to stand in the dark. Many were getting lost and disappearing into the darkness. The lamp holder didn't seem too concerned. To him it was like every time another person reached the place where he was, it was a testimony to the fact that his light was working and that he was being successful in his duty. He hardly seemed to notice that there was still a great deal further to go up the trail.

Then I saw a second light emerge. This second lamp holder looked identical the first, except that he fanned and fed his flame and planted his lamp post about fifty yards further up the path from where the first one was. Many of those who couldn't seem to fit in the light of the first lamp holder pressed on and found a place in the light of the next.

There was a third lamp holder who emerged from the crowd which had formed around the second man. This man also stepped out from the procession and planted his lamp post another fifty yards further up the path. And again, many of those who couldn't fit in the light of the first or the second headed off to the third.

These three lamp holders had such a look of valor, might and commitment. Just by looking at them I could tell that they had determined never to abandon their post night or day no matter what it took. Their light was their entire focus in life. They stood there with their glorious light shining brightly as beacons of the kingdom of God. With the amount of light given off from their lamps, there seemed to be enough area illuminated for a good percentage of the procession to survive in relative health.

BIRDS FROM THE NORTH

At this time I noticed each person in the procession was carrying a bundle of objects. At first I couldn't tell what the objects were. But then the objects became clearer and clearer. They took on the form of money, people, titles, buildings, and positions of power.

The Spirit said, "They are carrying their gifts and their callings. They are bringing them to the alter in the hill forest where they will offer them up to the Lord as a sacrifice of praise and thanksgiving."

But then I kept seeing these huge dark birds from the north that would swoop down and try to grab anything that was in the hands of the people. Some were able to successfully hide their gifts and callings from these dark birds, but many were not. The ones whom the birds were trying to raid had different reactions. For some, when the birds grabbed their bundle, they held on for a moment, but then as soon as they realized that the birds were dragging them away from the procession, they let go and fell back to the ground, not loosing too much of their progress up the path. But there were others who refused to let go, and because of this, they would get swept far away to wherever the birds were going.

The Spirit said, "These are the birds of prey—scavengers who try to feast upon the sacrifices to the Lord."

There had already been a great sacrifice made on behalf of the saints to carry these things as far as they had. Because of this, when the birds swooped down and grabbed hold of their gifts and callings, the pride in many of them refused to let go. As they did this, the birds would lift them too and begin to carry them away. They were being carried away by their attachment to their own gifts and callings.

The Spirit said, "They have begun to mistake the gift of God for the substance of God; to them the gifts and the callings of Christ have become more valuable than the Person of Christ. In their pride and ambition, when the season came, they failed to hide their gifts and callings. For this reason, they lost their sacrifice of praise and thanksgiving to God."

I realized as the birds carried them away, that in the natural world they might still look more successful than ever. But in the meantime, in spirit, their gifts and callings had now gone from something to be placed upon the altar of God into something that was actually distancing their hearts from God.

The Spirit continued, "There is no idolatry in the Kingdom of God. For this reason, God allows them to be tested in this way."

My attention now turned to those who had successfully hidden their gifts for this season and those who let go and had fallen back to the ground. At first, with empty hands, those who had let go all together moved very slowly with a type of humility. They walked along almost dragging their feet; they were desperately trying to accept and embrace the fact that they now had nothing to offer.

TWO SOURCES OF SUFFERING

Then after a short time, I saw a different set of birds emerge in a beautiful pattern from the forest. As they came closer I could see that they were doves. They were very gentle and soft. They would come from the forest, and gently descend and fall upon all those who had hidden or given up their gifts and callings. As they did this, a new bundle would begin to grow in the hands of the people. This new bundle grew larger and larger and brighter and brighter. Soon the latter bundle far exceeded the former bundle in size and glory.

The Spirit said, "The gifts and the callings of God are without repentance, yet humility must precede power for those who would enter the kingdom. Humility is often learned best through failure."

He continued, "Many of the greatest saints within your generation are those whom the Lord has set apart to receive their greatest anointing by suffering through failure. Yet those who are faithful till the end will receive a crown of life."

I began thinking, "But God doesn't send suffering to us, does He?"

The Spirit answered, "God does not send suffering as much as He *is* suffering. Love is long-suffering. For this reason you cannot experience the depths of Gods love without opportunities to suffer long. It is not that He enjoys watching you suffer, but that He enjoys watching you love. There are two main sources of the sufferings of this age, love and sin. At the bottom of *all* suffering though is a doorway that opens into a realm of union with Him, the depths of which you would never know without the fellowship of sufferings."

He continued, "Nevertheless, I say to you that suffering in the sense that you think of it will pass away along with all your enemies at the end of the age. But in the meantime, suffering is what we all must partake in as this age hangs on the scales of the knowledge of good and evil.

It seemed like He was saying that many within our generation will be tested in the area of their own gifts and callings. He was saying that those who have power and influence, those who have command of many people, such as managers, pastors and professionals, will be tested with their own prosperity like Job to see whether or not these objects which are intended for sacrifice and praise have become idols.

BEELZEBUB

There was another thing moving in the skies far off to the north. It looked like a snow man made of three big snowballs, holding on to something that looked like a big black umbrella. As it got closer, I found it was actually a big black bird, like a crow. As it approached and began to pass over high above the procession, the snowman released and dropped its entire bottom section like an egg falling from a hen. When it hit the ground, it split open and multitudes of little white alien-looking monsters burst out. Immediately they ran over and began climbing up the backs of the people in the procession. They would move into a position where they could perch on the shoulders of the person. Then they would slowly burrow their needle like noses through the persons hair and like a mosquito they would pierce their noses into the backs of their skulls! They were like giant albino ticks, as their entire heads were disappearing into the heads of these people.

It seemed like even though these little monsters had managed to burrow their head through the skull of a person, some of them were not finding anything to eat. After a few moments, they would shrivel up and fall on the ground and die. Others seemed to find many things to eat for they were growing larger and larger and more and more secure in their place.

Within the head of each person, when the little white monsters found something good for eating, they would first throw up their own stomach acid on it and let it breakdown and dissolve the specific area of the person's brain. It was just like a fly. Once the portion of the person's mind had become liquefied enough to drink, they would then slurp it up. However, it wasn't but a moment before they would again throw up their stomach acid into what was now a void in the persons mind. The regurgitated substance would now infect and begin to decay an even larger portion of the mind. Then again, when it was ready, they would slurp it up. Over and over they did this. Every time, their bodies would expand in size, and an increasing amount of the person's mind became acidified. It seemed like they were intending to do this until the entire brain was theirs.

The Spirit said, "The snowman is Beelzebub. He is the lord of the flies. He is the keeper of the river of lust."

He continued, "If there is nothing to eat, there is nothing to regurgitate. But if he finds something to eat, he will eat it and spit it back in order to infect the other parts of the mind which otherwise could have been used positively."

I looked closer at the little creatures. On their backs they were carrying a pouch of eggs. It wasn't as much that they were hungry, but they were preparing a place to hatch their eggs. If the little monsters found something big enough in the mind of a person, after they had regurgitated it a few times and turned enough of the persons mind to liquid lust, they would plant an egg. Over time, the egg would hatch and many little monsters would begin to feed like maggots upon the brain.

The Spirit said, "They are liars."

STARTING OVER IS NOT ALWAYS A WASTE OF TIME

At first, the people who were infected seemed to have no clue these hideous monsters were feasting on their brains. But soon, many of them began to realize something was wrong. They began to look fearful, desperate, and depressed. They began crying out to God.

The Spirit spoke out to them, "Confess! Return to the light!"

Upon hearing this, many of them immediately turned and headed back into the gate of the castle where the light in the courtyard had previously cleansed them. But there were many who didn't go back. To those who didn't go back, it didn't make sense to go all the way back to the castle. After all, it was the opposite direction of the procession. In my own mind I also thought it was a mistake to return to the castle. This seemed too risky—even the opposite of spiritual progress.

The Spirit said, "You cannot walk in faith when you are conscious of sin. You cannot progress any further in His righteousness if you continue to maintain sin consciousness."

This time as I looked at these people, I could see that they were only half cleansed. After the stone man had thrown them, and they landed in front of the light, they only let it see one side of them. They did not allow it to cleanse all of them. They had hidden certain things the first time they passed through the light and now they were bound by these dark secrets. These secrets were the very things the little monsters fed upon.

The Spirit said, "Many of those in your generation have not allowed themselves to be fully seen by the Light. Because of this, they cannot fully see the Light. They can only come so far. Their darkness will not permit them to pass any further."

Their darkness was like an invisible chain, which only allowed them to go so far from the castle. I saw that those who chose to go back to the castle had already arrived and were presently being cleansed. I watched as a few of them came to the star of Light. As the Light hit them, the little monsters fell to the ground with a shriek, then shriveled up into dust.

It was surprising to me that those who returned were now already heading back, and they had almost come to the place where they had been previously. It was almost as if they had not lost any time in the whole process.

For those who would not return to the Light in the gate, I saw that there was a huge battle going on within them. They were not going back because they didn't want to give up the progress they had made in coming this far. There was a great fear of failure and they linked failure with starting over.

The Spirit said, "It's not a waste to start over. Without the death of certain things, there can be no life within those same things. Unless a grain of wheat falls into the ground and dies, it remains alone; but if it dies, it bears much fruit. Without going back to expose certain things, there often can be no further progress, only spent time."

After I had thought of this for a moment, the Spirit said, "There are others whom I have already made clean who are also going back to live at the courtyard. This too is folly."

As He said this I saw many meandering back near the castle. They had been totally cleansed, but they were not advancing. They were not going to the river, they were not doing anything. They were just standing there. I wondered why they would not come back up the hill.

The Spirit said, "False humility and a lack of discipline."

These people had come to believe that since their first attempt up the hill didn't work out, somehow the procession was not really true. Although they knew they were out of the castle and could see the procession with their eyes, they convinced themselves that the procession had been just an illusion all along. In their pride they seemed to be saying that since they were not able to make it up the hill, there is no way anyone else could.

For these, when the suggestion first came that they might need to go back, it became shame to them. No one had ever discipled them in humility to fight for the promises and high calling that God had placed on them. Therefore, they didn't know how to deal with failure and humiliation. This failure and humiliation now turned into shame, and the shame was covered with a false humility.

The Spirit said, "False humility can be seen by its placement upon others."

By this I believe the Spirit was saying that true humility does not compare itself to others. It acts purely out of obedience to Christ and it does not assume that anyone else will act the same way. True humility doesn't care if it is not served—only that it itself is serving. True humility is not concerned if others are not willing to serve, only that it is always willing. But false humility compares and competes. It is the kind where if you are doing something humble, you look at others and think of how unholy they are if they are not doing the same thing as you.

This is what those who would not rejoin the procession were doing. As they had advanced up the hill in the procession the first time and been denied because of their sin, instead of repenting and trying again, they told themselves that going up the mountain was prideful and that they should not try to come up there again. In essence, they said to themselves, I will stay back here at the place of humility and repentance because this is the only holy place to be, and it is pride that makes those people think they could become that close to God.

The Spirit seemed to be grieved by this.

Chapter 10

Death & His
Wagon of Compromise

THEN I HEARD SOMETHING far away. It was behind me to the south. I turned and saw on the horizon beyond the lamp holders a pitch-black covered wagon coming closer and closer to where I was.

The Spirit said, "The name of the one who drives this wagon is Death. He is disguised as provision."

A CONVERSATION WITH DEATH

As Death passed me with his covered wagon, he turned and looked at me as if he was surprised to see me there. He stopped his wagon and began to speak to me.

He said, "Those who are still on the path of the procession have not yet entered any kingdom; they have only come out from one and seen another. I have authority to trade freely with all on this path."

When Death first approached, he didn't seem to notice me. I was hoping that he might pass right by without issue but as soon as he got within a few yards his head snapped toward me in such a way that I knew I was the object of his full attention. When he first had noticed me, for a split second, it almost looked like he was startled by me. In that moment, he looked a bit like a child who just got caught doing something he knew he shouldn't be doing. But then when he saw I was terrified by him, his posture became much more threatening and intimidating. I was extremely distressed. I was horrified by his presence. It was as if time stood still. This experience was startling to me for a number of reasons.

Firstly, Death was very scary looking. He was a lightless black, like a black hole, always taking but never giving. There was no light or life reflected in him. He pulled all life in and released none. He was so void that it was as if he was permanently sucking all the light and life out of everything around him. I looked at him as a child might look upon someone who is severely deformed—with a pulling curiosity and fascination—not as much in order to discover the source of beauty, but more to discover the depths of deformity. He seemed to pull all the perversion out of me.

Secondly, I was startled because when he passed by, he spoke to me personally, and I was hoping that Death might not be able to see me.

The Spirit said, "This is a big problem with your generation because you have come to underestimate him."

After a moment, He continued, "More importantly, you have come to underestimate yourself."

After a another pause, He continued again, "But most of all you have come to underestimate Me."

He was saying we have come to underestimate the demonic realm; the demonic realm has much more power and influence than we give it credit for. He was also saying that we have come to underestimate ourselves; that we as children of the living God have much more power and influence over the spiritual realm then we have given ourselves credit for. But more than both of these, we have come to underestimate the power of God; we have failed in many ways to recognize the magnitude of His absolute power, authority and sovereignty.

Thirdly, this whole thing startled me because, as Death spoke to me, I was suddenly aware I was not just seeing in the spirit but actually was in the spirit. Because of this, it was not just the Holy Spirit that could see and hear me, but that all beings within the landscape of this realm could see and hear me.

As I stood there petrified, Death began to stare straight at me as if he were reading every thought and fear I had in my heart. This made me feel exceedingly afraid. At this moment I realized that this realm could see a lot more of me than I could see of it. I knew there were beings of much greater sight than I. In this realm my sight was so inexperienced that I could only see little in comparison.

As Death stared at me I began to feel more and more naked and bare as if I were alone in a desert with no clothes. Death was coming closer and closer to me. I became frantic and searched for a place to hide. My first thought was to run back into the castle. How could I though? This would be so wrong. As Death grew closer, so did the urge to hide. I had a second thought; build a shelter. But when I began to look around for something to build it with, I began to feel as if I was committing an act of treason.

I heard the Spirit say in a faint far away voice, "Return to Me."

Upon hearing the Holy Spirit's distant voice, I realized I had left the place of His presence out of intimidation and fear of Death. I immediately rushed back to the place I was previously and there I stood naked in front of Death.

The Spirit said "Stay here with Me and wait."

At that moment I was reminded of my first impression of Death. He seemed to be just as concerned, and even worried, about me seeing him as I was about him seeing me. I saw fear in Death. I held the hand of the Spirit of life in Christ and decided to stare right back at him. This frustrated Death because he could no longer intimidate or drive fear into me. So he eventually gave up and headed toward the people in the procession.

The Holy Spirit said, "His only power is the power you have allowed him to take. Greater is He who is in you than he who is in the world."

BREACHING THE PROCESSION

After leaving me, Death rode up in his covered wagon and stopped right behind one of the lamp holders who was lighting the path. No one seemed to notice him.

Death was very cautious as he neared the lamp holders. The way he approached made it seem like he feared and respected their light. It was as if the light was creating some sort of invisible force field that Death was not able to breach. As long as the lamp holders kept their eyes forward and their lights held high, they were solid and the procession was protected.

I noticed there were a number of other smaller lamp holders between the three big ones. The three stood as giants among all the others.

The Spirit said, "For a time I have called these three to represent the three pillars of all the lamp holders. The name of the first is Peace, the second, Truth, and the third, Righteousness."

But then Death began whispering to the first of the lamp holders. Peace stood strong at first, but after time fear, then doubt consumed him. He began to question what was going on behind his back. His eyes looked down and to the side. As soon as this happened, his grip loosened, his composure slouched, his countenance broke and the lamp post became too heavy to hold upright. It came crashing down. Peace was the first to break ranks and commence trade with Death.

As soon as the lamp post came crashing down Death shouted, "WAR." It was as if a black bomb of death went off, and all who were within the radius of about twenty feet fell down and were covered in a black tar-like substance. The people were scattered.

Death then moved on to the second lamp holder, Truth. The same thing happened except this time when Truth's lamp post crashed to the ground, Death shouted out, "HUMANISM!" Another bomb of death had gone off, and the people were scattered.

Death moved on to the third lamp holder, Righteousness. And again, the same thing happened. But when this lamp post crashed to the ground,

Death shouted out, "ADULTERY!" Another bomb of death went off and the people were scattered.

Where the lamp holders once stood with a light to show the way, there now stood three black tar-covered pillars of death. The people were scattered. One of the hardest things about this whole experience for the lamp holders was that their weaknesses had become exposed. After a while, the three lamp holders gathered their strength, began to pick up their tar covered lights, and tried to shine again. But now, the tar-like substance seemed to block out much of their former light. Their lights were greatly dimmed. Many of the people could only see that the lamp holders had failed. To many, they had become a reverse sign—a symbol of whom not to follow. The procession was now scattered; many had become angry and distraught. The three pillars now stood as symbols of Death's superiority and power. At this point, darkness was all around. One could hear screams and cries in the dark as Death had almost complete freedom to roam without being seen.

All hope had been lost. The procession was totally scattered with some going to the left, some going to the right, and some going back to the castle. No one was advancing. The entrance to the forest was so close. However, there was no light for the procession to see how to get there. Many began to despair and believe that since these three pillars had fallen, the way was blocked for them.

I was so angry at these lamp holders. How could they be such hypocrites? How could God give them such responsibility when they were only going to fail? I thought to myself that we all would have been better off without those three big lamp holders who took it upon themselves to shine the light for us. I could tell I was projecting every fatherly failure from my own birth father and my own church fathers onto these three lamp holders. I allowed my frustration to rage within my heart.

"Bastard fathers!" I cried out. "Where is my inheritance when I need it? Where is my protection when I need it most?"

The Spirit said, "You must rid yourself of this pride and rage before you can come into the glory that has been prepared for you."

As He said this, my rage was instantly stilled. It wasn't gone, but it was still enough for me to realize that He was talking not just to me, but to my entire generation, and to the procession. For the first time I understood that I was not only watching the procession, but I was one of them.

A NEW WAY OF WALKING

Like the procession, I wanted so badly to move forward but forward was the only path I could not find. With the procession, I was stuck blaming and lamenting over the lack of inheritance that had been passed down to me and to the church as a whole. There was such a lack of true spiritual discipleship. We knew so little of God. How could we even think to ever enter His Kingdom? We can't even walk in a procession! Again I felt the rage surge within, like my heart was about to burst with frustration and anger.

The Spirit reminded me again, "With man it is impossible, but with God all things are possible." - Matthew 19:26

I didn't really want to hear that. I wasn't in the mood for believing in God's providence unless I could see how He was going to provide. I was so tired of believing without seeing. I wanted to see the way past this mess.

"You must learn to walk by faith and not by sight," He said quoting 2 Corinthians 5:7.

After He said this I had no response, and everything was quiet for a long time. Sobriety and stillness now filled the air.

The Spirit again came to me. This time, He didn't speak to me, He just came close—closer than I had ever felt Him before. His love pierced me. It came in waves like knives that were carving off every layer of bitterness, blame, frustration and rage.

Then He said, "I AM your provision. I AM your inheritance"

As He said this, overwhelming emotion flooded over me and I fell to the ground and began to weep. I could hear what sounded like a million other people doing the same. The rest of the procession had heard the very same words I had heard, and they were responding in the same way.

After some time had passed, the Spirit again spoke, "I have been your covering; I have been your inheritance from the beginning of time."

His kindness seemed to kill me. I looked back over my life and realized I had sensed His presence with me at all times, pulling me closer to Him at every turn. I felt so ashamed and so unworthy, like my body and soul could not survive at this level of mercy and kindness. There was too much favor. I was embarrassed at my blindness. I was embarrassed that I had not recognized His presence before. I was embarrassed that I had ever blamed anyone for anything. I began to repent and ask forgiveness for my ignorance, for mankind's ignorance and for the Church's ignorance for how little we recognized His presence with us, His nearness, His provision, His protection. His inheritance. I hated the fact that I had earlier blamed those three lamp holders who were trying to shine their light for me. I heard the rest of the procession also weeping and repenting.

After a long time of processing the interaction, utter peace came. We all felt humbled, without anxiety or stress about our future. If we had Him, what else did we need? We didn't need to get anywhere. There was no rush unless He was in a rush. But He wasn't so we were fine. We all just laid there in total surrender as the Holy Spirit sent waves of grace and peace to wash over us.

After many hours of being refreshed in the presence of the Holy Spirit, He said, "Arise and see!"

I got up and looked, and even though it was quite dark, I could see movement again in the procession. Where previously so many in the procession had been laid out on the ground in repentance and grace, some were beginning to stand up again and form a new line. The smaller lamp holders who formerly stood under the three were the first to stand, and now they had moved over to give light to a new path right next to the first one. As light hit, I could tell this path actually wasn't new at all. In fact it seemed much older and more worn then the path they had just come from. It was narrower than the previous path and it was overgrown with grass, but it had been there all along. No one seemed to have noticed it until now.

The Spirit said, "They have found the path of the overcomer."

Judging by the tone of the Spirit, I got the impression that we had come to an extremely important subject to Him—one that moved Him deeply. It was the subject of overcoming.

I remembered the scripture, "He who overcomes will inherit these things and I will be his God and he will be My son." - Revelation 21:7

Chapter 11

The New Lamp Holders

IT WAS OBVIOUS NOW that it had been the Spirit's plan all along to bring people onto this path. I began to think about how many things had had to happen for everyone to get to the place they now were. I thought about all the trials everyone in the procession had gone through. At the beginning of every trial was a sense of despair and abandonment, as if everyone had been forgotten by God. But in the end, every trial was shown merely to be a stepping stone of advancement. Every new trial was an opportunity to manifest our destiny.

THE POWER OF TRIALS AND PERSECUTION

The Spirit said, "Trials perfect their students. External trials are merely opportunities for internal victories to be revealed. The Lord always disciplines those He loves." The Spirit said this, partially quoting Hebrews 12:6.

I thought of Christ and the scripture in Hebrews 2:10.   It says, "For it was fitting for Him, for whom are all things, and through whom are all things, in bringing many sons to glory, to perfect the Author of their salvation through sufferings."

I believe the Spirit was saying that just as Christ had to suffer to become who He was in us, we must also partake in certain sufferings to become who we are in Him. Suffering is essential for all sons to be made perfect and mature. Without it, much of our inheritance is forfeited.

I also remembered Romans 8:16-17, "The Spirit himself testifies with our spirit that we are God's children. Now if we are children, then we are heirs—heirs of God and co-heirs with Christ, if indeed we share in his sufferings in order that we may also share in his glory."

And Philippians 3:10-11, "I want to know Christ and the power of his resurrection and the fellowship of sharing in his sufferings, becoming like him in his death, and so, somehow, to attain to the resurrection from the dead."

The Spirit said, "If you will share in His resurrection, you must also share in His crucifixion."

As I meditated on these passages, I realized they were not necessarily saying that we have to partake in our own sufferings, but in Christ's. That is, we must suffer our former life to crucifixion and recon ourselves crucified with Him. While I loved this revelation, my mind couldn't stop thinking of those who are suffering in a different way. I was wondering about those who are dealing with the hardships of starvation, war, disease and famine. Was there a difference between suffering this type of trail, or even the trials of everyday life, than with suffering persecution or reproach for the sake of Christ?

The Spirit said, "Trials have been given to all for the sake of perfection. Persecution has been given to some for the sake of glory. If you will share in His perfection, you must overcome its trials. If you will share in His glory, you must overcome its persecutions."

I thought to myself, "How could we share in the sufferings and persecutions of Christ in America? There is no persecution here."

The Spirit responded, "Yes there is—if you obey Me."

He continued, "If you are unashamed of My kingdom and My gospel, you will be persecuted. Indeed, all who desire to live godly in Christ

Jesus will be persecuted. Yet, these present sufferings are not worth comparing with the glory that will be revealed in you." (Quoting 2 Tim 3:12 and Romans 8:18)

He continued again, "The first mountain that you must overcome is the mountain that stands in the way of faith, hope and love. If you have these, you will not be ashamed, you will not fear, and you will never lack power to proclaim My good news. Yet overcoming does not always mean worldly victory. Overcoming means never ceasing to maintain faith, hope and love. In the eyes of the world, these often appear to be the opposite of victory. Yet for those who are inheriting the kingdom of God, these in themselves are the victory. This is the victory of Christ on His cross."

I thought about how even though Christ seemed to be defeated as He died upon the cross, He maintained His faith, hope and love till the end, He was proven victorious by the resurrection from the dead. I wondered how many people and organizations were out there who were fighting the very thing that could be their victory; crucifixion. I remembered the scripture, "Let us fix our eyes on Jesus, the author and perfecter of our faith, who for the joy set before Him endured the cross, scorning its shame, and sat down at the right hand of the throne of God. Consider Him who endured such opposition from sinful men, so that you will not grow weary and lose heart." - Hebrews 2:2-3

The Spirit said, "You too must learn to overcome if you will inherit these things. Every trial is a potential perfection, every suffering a potential glory."

THE NEW LAMP HOLDERS

After considering what had just been said, my focus turned again to the procession and its newly revealed path. At first, there were only a few of the small lamp holders lighting the path. Many of the other small lamp holders had stood, but they did not go yet to the new trail. They seemed to be preoccupied. As I got a better look, I could see they were making more lamps —thousands of them! Then the lamp holders began recruiting thousands of the people within the procession by giving them their own lamps. Not only did they give them their own lamps, but they taught those in the procession how to make more. The number of them grew so much that soon all those who had light were touching each other. The light from their lamp posts grew brighter and brighter until it far exceeded the light given previously from the three.

I had the impression that the previous three fallen lamp holders represented church leadership.

The Spirit said, "Yes, but this is not revealing as much how the Lord has seen, but how the world is seeing."

Thinking back to the original three lamp holders, I realized I had received a picture of what Death has brought much of the world into believing about the church and its pastors, priests and reverends. There have been so many high profile Christian leaders who have fallen into sex scandals, or bowed to humanism, or succumbed to strife, bloodshed and war throughout the last 1000 years. As a result, the world can't help but see the institutional church as a sign of where not to go—a sign of death.

I did not sense that the Spirit was trying to place blame or fault on any individual, or on the church as a whole. Nor was He saying He was no longer going to work within the institutional church. In fact I got the sense that were it not for the three lamp holders, no one would have made it this far.

The Spirit said, "They were never meant to be an end, only a means to the end goal which is Christ."

The former trail only led so far. It could not bring people any further than the lamp holders themselves. And now that it had become so dark and indistinguishable, a new trail was beginning to be forged. The church was now changing into something parallel and in the same direction, but different than it had been previously. It seemed like the Spirit was indicating that this change was good, and in a way it was what He always intended. I wanted to go back and think about all the details of what I saw.

First, I remembered was that the new lamp holders were so much smaller than the previous three. In fact, most of them were even much smaller than the people in the procession.

The Spirit said, "These are familiar with the lowest and smallest things."

As He said this, the passage in Matthew 20:25-28 came to mind. It says, "But Jesus called them to Himself and said, 'You know that the rulers of the Gentiles lord it over them, and their great men exercise authority over them. It is not this way among you, but whoever wishes to become great among you shall be your servant, and whoever wishes to be first among you shall be your slave; just as the Son of Man did not come to be served, but to serve, and to give His life a ransom for many.'"

I was instantly struck with my own pride. I remembered the many times that in my pride, I had assumed I was spiritually superior to all those around me. I loved their need for my light. I thought of all the times when in my pride I insisted upon being heard more than hearing. The contentment to practice the nameless service that these small lamp holders possessed made me feel ashamed and embarrassed about my desires for popularity and recognition. I could see they always seemed to find the lowest places to serve. They didn't care if they were paid for it or not. They didn't care if they had titles or not. To these saints, if they were not in the lowest place, they almost didn't feel like Christ was there with them. They were not against other believers or church leaders being placed upon big platforms or high places. In fact, they often were the ones who enabled them to get there. However, they themselves never felt comfortable being one of them.

I couldn't help but think that the Holy Spirit was saying through this that He was intending to promote those who were poor in spirit as the next generation of church leaders.

He said, "The meek shall inherit the earth."

Secondly, I remembered how the new lamp holders were more numerous than the previous three. It seemed like He was showing a move of God upon the church to raise up hundreds of anointed servant leaders in the place of a few, and that church leadership would slowly be moving from a few of the mighty, to many of the meek.

Here I questioned, "Doesn't God want His church leaders to be bold, strong and courageous? How does meekness fit in?"

The Spirit said, "Meekness is not weakness. It is the opposite. Meekness is when one has all the power and all the strength to do what they want, but then they choose to exhibit their strength by submitting it to another. This is meekness. Jesus is meekness. You (meaning our generation) must learn meekness."

As I looked back at the procession, the Spirit spoke up again, "They shall be a kingdom of priests to our God; and they will reign upon the earth." (Quoting Revelation 5:10)

He seemed to emphasize how every individual within the procession was to be given a lamp and to be considered a priest who would enter the holy place to make sacrifices to the Lord.

From this, I thought about how often in times past the church placed its identity primarily in a small group of key leaders or founding fathers, and spiritual contribution in the church was generally limited only to the very few. If someone couldn't fit under the umbrella of one leader's light, they were forced to try to find another leader's light. This resulted in feelings of failure and inadequacy on both sides, which in turn resulted in offense, competition, and spiteful division. The way the former path was functioning was still allowing much room for the way of the castle to prevail.

I believe the Spirit was indicating that not only had the function of the former path become a source of needless division but it had become a source of great loss. Because people never learned they could carry the light of Christ on their own, they were restricted to go only as far as the lamp holders' lights permitted. Instead of the Spirit of Christ, they had become dependent upon man. This caused the procession to move very slowly if at all.

The Spirit said, "Will you make room for My anointing to come upon all My priests?"

As He asked this, I thought about all of the times I had seen the Spirit quenched because of heavy-handed or controlling leaders. I thought about all the times I saw leaders manipulate the church out of fear and control, not allowing members to do as the Spirit led them. So many were motivated out of fear of losing influence in their ministry to someone else, rather than being genuinely excited about the Kingdom of God expanding. I began to wonder how many decisions throughout church history had been made out of genuine faith as opposed to fear and control. The separation of laity and clergy started seeming like a really big issue to me. I wondered if God ever intended there to be any separation at all? It almost felt like separation to any degree was wrong.

If I could gather anything from all of this, it was that the single pastor, priest, or minister, who in days past performed the entire worship service, might now expect to accommodate an influx of believers who long to enter the throne room of grace to offer a contribution to the Lord along side of them. People were going to get the revelation of their own role and authority in the kingdom. The balance of power and authority was going to begin to shift from a few of the mighty to many of the meek.

DISCIPLESHIP

Thirdly, I remembered the new lamp holders were given the power to make more lamps. And they were recruiting common people thus multiplying their numbers rapidly.

The Spirit said, "You must go and make disciples of every nation teaching them to observe all the things I have commanded you and I will be with you always even till the end of the age." (Partially quoting Matthew 28:19-20)

I became convicted about the church of this generation. Some, it seems, have learned how to carry the light of Christ on their own, but few could say they have truly learned how to impart the light of Christ to others. I myself had learned how to study my bible and preach under the anointing of the Holy Spirit. But our survival as a church seems now to depend more on my ability to carry this big light than upon Christ. I wondered if I had taught anyone how to create their own lamp so they could see the path of Christ on their own.

I remembered the scripture in 1 John 2:27. It seemed like the Holy Spirit was speaking this over the procession and our generation. "As for you, the anointing which you received from Him abides in you, and you have no need for anyone to teach you; but as His anointing teaches you about all things, and is true and is not a lie, and just as it has taught you, you abide in Him."

God wants us to teach each one to learn how to make and carry lights of their own. He wants everyone to learn that they have a right to be ministers empowered by the Holy Spirit not just to come to His church on occasion, but to be His church wherever they go!

The Spirit was now showing a better way. It is perhaps more costly because one's own light in many ways may have to diminish for a time, but in the end it will result in a greater light overall. If we are not willing to forsake our own life for the sake of the whole, what is the whole worth?

The Spirit said, "The Kingdom of God cannot be fully expressed in the life of an individual until that individual accepts their oneness with all its members."

As He said this, I remembered the scripture in John 17:22-23. It says, "The glory which You have given Me I have given to them, that they may be one, just as We are one; I in them and You in Me, that they may be perfected in unity, so that the world may know that You sent Me, and loved them, even as You have loved Me."

I believe the Spirit was saying if anyone wants to mature in the Kingdom of God, they must first learn that Christ made them one with all the rest. The only way forward is in union. If they are not willing to see and move as one, than there is no way forward. Every last individual needs to offer their contribution if we as a whole will come to our destiny. We must learn to make lights and place them in the hands of others until everyone has their own!

Fourthly, I remembered the smaller lamp holders were all touching.

The Spirit said, "They are touchable."

As He said this, I thought of all the times I, along with so many other leaders I knew, had been unwilling to be truly touched by others. I thought of how many times I had seen pastors hide behind their pulpits, saying things in public that they would never say face to face. I wondered how many leaders were actually truly known by anyone at all. The Spirit seemed to be saying that He was appointing a generation of leaders who are willing to have their lives touched by the lowly—touched by commoners.

The Spirit said, "Christ became touchable because He saw treasure in you. Are you willing to become touchable for the treasure He sees in them?"

I felt a little discouraged. To be honest, I didn't know if I really wanted to be "touchable."

"You have yet to fully die and let Christ truly live in you?" He said, questioning me.

"Yes, I guess so." I thought to myself. "But then how come you are showing me this truth if I am not willing to walk in it?" I asked.

"I am showing you what could be. I am showing you where you could go." He said.

He continued, "Many people say they want to experience the Kingdom of God but they forget that the Kingdom of God is made of people. They also forget that the Kingdom of God is hostile to all other kingdoms—especially their own."

I thought of the passage of scripture that says, "Suppose one of you wants to build a tower. He will first sit down and estimate the cost to see whether he has enough money to finish it, won't he? Otherwise, if he lays a foundation and can't finish the building, everyone who watches will begin to ridicule him and say, 'This person started a building but couldn't finish it.' Or suppose a king is going to war against another king. He will first sit down and consider whether with 10,000 men he can oppose the one coming against him with 20,000 men, won't he? If he can't, he will send a delegation to ask for terms of peace while the other king is still far away. In the same way, none of you can be my disciple unless he gives up all his possessions." -Luke 14:27-33

I sat quiet for a while considering what had been said. I began to think of how the last thing I saw was the way the light the new procession emitted grew far greater than its former glory. The Spirit seemed to be indicating that if we are to move forward in the Kingdom and glory of God, these changes must first take place.

THE SCEPTER OF DEATH

All of a sudden I realized that I had lost track of where Death had gone. As I turned to look, I saw that the procession had reassembled and was looking stronger than they had ever looked previously. Death was approaching the procession, and he looked a bit confused about whom he should attack. Eventually he chose one and tried to speak to him. As he did this, all the other lamp holders in the nearby area immediately surrounded him and shoved their lamps in the face of Death. Death snarled in anger and backed away. Death chose another member of the procession to try and crack but again, the lamp holders banded together and shut him out. The lamp holders were so numerous and so tight that Death could not even come close to breaking a single one of them, much less the growing thousands of them. Death backed off and, returning to his wagon, he sat down and stared back at the procession. I could tell he was thinking and trying to come up with a different strategy.

Death had been carrying a scepter with a tip that was shaped like a magnet at the end. Up to this point I hadn't seen him use it, but at this point he rose out of the wagon, circled around and stood between the horse and all the rest of the people. From here he stretched out his scepter and began sweeping swiftly through the crowd touching every person he could. The scepter looked like it was made of ice and metal. It reminded me of the steady and gradual pull of the castle's river, but this scepter seemed to hold all the power and draw of the entire river in one condensed blow. It stunned whomever it touched. For most of those who were hit by the scepter, their eyes would instantly turn inward.

The Spirit said, "The scepter's name is Self."

It caused all its victims' hearts to become like Death, an inward black hole, their minds as a thought magnet, sucking every thought inward and making it about self. His scepter always went before him and as it struck each person, their eyes became self centered. They would enter a frantic survivor mentality thus thinking of themselves as independent from the group.

Many of the people who were hit by the scepter now stood aside and drew a circle on the ground. Their focus turned toward keeping all the ground they had gained so far. They stopped thinking of going any further. They became a source unto themselves, an island of self. They began looking somewhat greedily at the procession, the castle, and the river. They took on the attitude and look of the vendors who traded on the banks of lust. Yet instead of money, they traded attention. They competed to become the thing that the procession was attracted to most. They didn't care where they set up shop so long as they could do their business. The castle, the river, and the procession all became the same to them.

Those who were touched by the scepter now took on the properties of a magnet. Their negative polarity pushed away all those that would not be controlled while their positive polarity drew those who would. Just as magnets have opposite polarities, each one who was touched became forcibly moved to a place where no one could come close to help or touch. The only ones who could come were the ones who themselves had not been touched or who had, but the sting had had small effect. These were almost always sucked in and then used and manipulated to fit into the ones own use for them. It was a tragedy because almost always the stronger the following became, the more isolated they were forced to become.

Many of these were true church men who began the procession with the best intentions, but as they got out in the open and were hit by the scepter of Death, they instantly resorted back to their former securities and to what they knew they could do—this was to build walls. Many of these were once great men who moved speedily and helped others to do the same in the procession. But now they had stopped all progress in the procession and were only trying to gather as many as possible to their polarity. They worked their vending booths and often sold their services to the highest bidder in order to gain their own security.

The Spirit said, "Compromise is the merchandise of Death. He has an abundance of it. He sells it to become rich."

Death had very good deals. Deals that almost always looked much better to us than to continue in the procession. He was a Socratic salesman— able to question our current course with great effectiveness and influence demonstrating why we need his product so badly. Death's product took on any form he wanted, but it was empty. He loved it. Every time he stopped another person, it created a greater obstacle for the rest of the procession to try to maneuver around.

Rage and frustration welled up inside me and I began to try to come up with a way to kill Death.

The Spirit said, "He is already dead. That is his name. This is his misery. Death is not the end of existence, but a form of existence. When one is dead in spirit, it is not that their spirit is non-existent; it is that their spirit is under the government of Death. Death is a being who governs. All of those spirits under his government exist and are governed by the spirit of Death."

I noticed that Death always tended to face toward the graveyard away from the hill and the white horse. I realized that his power was in his ability to turn eyes away from the white horse.

All of a sudden panic hit me in my stomach as I realized I was one of those who was turned away from the forest. In fact I had never even faced it yet, I just found myself standing with my back to it. I too had been hit with the scepter of Death and I too had partaken of compromise. That is why I was not moving. I turned to face the Spirit and the forest and as I did I was blinded by a Light.

In that moment a beautiful voice spoke out to me from the great Light and said, "Come, I must show you your beginning."

Chapter 12

The Beginning of Man

I KNEW WHEN THE SPIRIT SAID, "I must show you your beginning," He wasn't talking about me singularly. He was speaking plurally.

He said, "Yes, you, as in mankind."

Suddenly, I was seeing myself in a moving picture. It was like the Holy Spirit had put me inside a television set that was taking me back in time, showing me the movie of our history. It was not just singular pictures anymore, but now much more like a motion picture of our past.

THE MAN & THE DRAGON

The movie began with me up on the same grassy hill where I was standing when I had originally seen the first picture of this vision. The forest was behind me and to the left, but there was no castle nor river mote in the field below. It was just a plain grassy field. It was beautiful.

Then I saw in slow motion a bolt of lightning surging through the sky, carrying in its branches a creature that looked like a small dragon, but had the stature of a man. He came crashing down onto the field where the castle had been.

Shortly after, I saw what looked like a normal man falling more gently and land in the same field, close to the dragon. After the man had landed, he stood up and began looking at his surroundings.

Immediately, I heard the Holy Spirit's old soft voice call to him from the forest behind me.

Hearing the voice, the man turned and noticed the forest on the hill which was just past where I was standing. It seemed like, as the Spirit spoke to him, he experienced a type of pleasure and love that greatly attracted him. As soon as the voice had begun to speak to him, he immediately began hurrying up towards the hill forest in excitement and expectation as if he knew something good was waiting for him there.

But before the man could take even a few steps, the dragon came directly up to him and stood between him and the forest and began to speak to him. At first the man was facing the dragon and the forest, which was behind the dragon's back. But as the dragon continued talking, the man slowly began turning, and soon the dragon was talking to the back of his head. At first, the man was recognizing the dragon as an individual, but the longer he listened to the dragon talk, the less he seemed to be able to discern the difference between his own voice and that of the dragon's. The man turning was like a sign that he had completely accepted the dragon's voice as his own and that he was no longer willing to see the dragon as an individual distinct from himself.

I wondered how it was possible for the man not to discern that the dragon's voice was different from his own.

The Spirit replied, "It is because he does not truly know himself."

I stood there wondering what he meant by this.

He continued, "As you heard Me speak to him just moments ago, he didn't know that My voice was any different from his own either. He just heard a voice and assumed it was his own. He does not truly know himself because he has never looked upon himself in the true mirror. The Word of

God is the true mirror. But since he has not yet looked into the Word, he does not yet know himself, nor does he know where he ends and the dragon begins. He knows almost no distinction between himself and his environment. Many people have fallen a great way. God has created man to subdue his environment; instead, man has been subdued by it."

I remembered the very first commandment God gave to Adam and Eve in Genesis 1:28 to rule over the entire created realm. He said, "Be fruitful, multiply, fill the earth, subdue the earth and rule over it." Yet I had never considered that our spiritual environment was included in this too.

As I remembered verses like Ephesians 6:12 which says, "For we wrestle not against flesh and blood, but against principalities, against powers, against the rulers of the darkness of this world, against spiritual wickedness in heavenly places." And 2 Corinthians 10:3-5 which says, "For though we walk in the flesh, we do not war after the flesh and the weapons of our warfare are not of the flesh, but divinely powerful for the pulling down of strongholds. Casting down speculations, and every high thing that exalts itself against the knowledge of God, and taking every thought captive to the obedience of Christ." I became convinced that God does indeed intend for us not only to subdue and rule over our natural environment, but our spiritual environment as well.

In Matthew 18:18-20 Jesus says, "Truly I tell you, whatever you bind on earth will have been bound in heaven, and whatever you loose on earth will have been loosed in heaven. Furthermore, truly I tell you that if two of you agree on earth about anything you request, it will be done for you by my Father in heaven. For where two or three have come together in my name, there I am in their midst."

I thought to myself that if God has truly given us authority to steward all natural and spiritual environments on the earth, it would also have to include angels and demons as well.

I was reminded of the verse that says, "Do you not know that we will judge the angels? How much more matters of this life?" (1 Corinthians 6:3) and the scripture that says, "The seventy returned with joy, saying, 'Lord, even the demons are subject to us in Your name.'" (Luke 10:17)

The Spirit said, "It is important that you understand the environment which you are seeing is the spiritual environment. This is the truest environment. All your life you have seen your physical world, now I am showing you a picture of your spiritual world. The spiritual world co-exists simultaneously with the material world. What you see is not material, but light. Light reveals truth. This principal is true of both worlds. There is much more light yet to be seen."

I began to think about light and how I perceive reality. I began to examine what the Spirit said about light and material and how our physical eyes are only physical organs that are designed to interpret light. I thought of how we also must have spiritual eyes that interpret light and darkness in the spiritual world.

Matthew 6:22-23 says, "The eye is the lamp of the body. So if your eye is healthy, your whole body will be full of light. But if your eye is evil, your whole body will be full of darkness. Therefore, if the light in you is darkness, how great is that darkness!"

The Spirit continued, "The spiritual leads the physical. God is Spirit and He relates to man in a spiritual environment. When man chooses the right spiritual environment, his material environment will naturally fall in line. Remember Adam."

He continued, "Many people in your generation think it divine to become one with their environment–as if their environment was the greater. But I say to you God never intended you to be mastered by His creation, but that His creation would be mastered by you. The earth will always be subject to her inhabitants, to man, for this is her design. She will always produce outwardly what the soul of man is manifesting inwardly. Man's environment will always be a sign that reveals the state of his soul. Your Creator has placed you as the crown of all creation, well equipped and worthy to rule. His creation longs and earnestly seeks to be led by you into His glory. When you allow yourself to become greedy and polluted in spirit, you fail earth in your role as her steward and you end up polluting the earth. It is not My will for you to become one with your environment, but that your environment is one with you. This is what I will restore to you."

As He said this, I remembered Romans 8:21, "The creation itself also will be set free from its slavery to corruption into the freedom of the glory of the children of God.

I also remembered Revelation 22:5, talking about the final restoration of man, "They shall reign for ever and ever."

HOW THE ISLAND OF ISOLATION BEGAN

After some time I noticed that the dragon was now speaking to the man like a puppet. As the dragon spoke, the man yielded and allowed himself to be pushed, pulled, and persuaded as if by his own will. The dragon convinced him to come over to a certain place in the field. It was quite easy for the dragon to control the man's movements because the man knew no difference between his own thoughts and those of the dragon.

When the dragon had taken the man to a certain place, he gave the man a pickaxe and pointed to a certain spot on the ground. The man swung and struck the ground and immediately a torrent of water burst forth flowing out from the one spot in two opposite directions. At first the man looked excited. For the first time, he felt what it was like to have power over something else, power to change his environment. He felt the power he was originally created to possess. With so little effort he had made such a huge impact on the land around him.

He hungrily sought to hear the next idea that came from the place the dragon occupied in his mind so he might experience this power again. This thought was interrupted however by the startling sight of the torrent of water which had now turned and was encircling him. Within seconds the water had come around full circle creating what was now an island on which he and the dragon were stuck. Where both the streams met, it looked like there was a siphon that sucked the waters down into the ground. The island that the water carved out was very long and narrow.

The Spirit said, "The man's name is Adam. The field he struck is Babylon and the Nations."

As he said this, my mind instantly filled with thoughts of Adam as we read of him in the Bible. He was the firstborn, and father, of all mankind.

I began to think about his relationship with the serpent and his fall and its consequences.

I also thought of Babylon. I turned to Revelation and found that Babylon was likened to a prostitute. This is what it said about her, "The angel also said to me, 'The waters you saw, on which the prostitute is sitting, are peoples, multitudes, nations, and languages. The ten horns and the beast you saw will hate the prostitute. They will leave her abandoned and naked... And so they will give their kingdom to the beast until God's words are fulfilled. The woman you saw is the great city that rules over the kings of the earth.'" - Revelation 17:15-18

The Spirit again spoke, "The dragon has very little power against purity, but when purity bows to deception, the dragon becomes purity's master. If purity is to survive here, it must also become as wise and as shrewd as the dragon."

I immediately thought of Matthew 10:16 which says, "Behold, I send you forth as sheep in the midst of wolves: be ye therefore wise as serpents, and as innocent as doves."

THE TEMPTATIONS OF BOREDOM AND LONELINESS

The man, now feeling scared and isolated, tried to see the dragon again as an individual. But the dragon had the strange ability to always stay behind Adam so that he could never see him. Adam felt fear, isolation and, for the first time bitterness. The dragon on the other hand seemed ecstatic. The dragon then jumped up upon Adam's shoulders and with his long sharp fingernails dug into his forehead and plied and pulled until Adam's scalp began to separate from his skull. The dragon pulled and cut until he had completely removed the scalp of Adam. He then threw it in the dirt, wove grass into it and placed it upon his own head as a crown. Blood and dirt dripped down the dragon's face and head as he laughed greedily. The dragon had taken the crown and covering of Adam, and crowned himself with it. He was crowning himself king of Adam and the island.

The Spirit said, "The dragon governs isolation which governs through deception."

Adam, now in pain, feeling wounded, naked, and without any protection, remembered the forest that he had seen at first and looked up desperately in a hope that he might at least be able to see that which had formerly made him feel so secure, so peaceful, and so free. But now as he looked up, the violent waters were creating so much mist that he could not resemble anything that looked even remotely familiar. Over the next several minutes, as the mist grew thicker and thicker, it eventually turned into a low lying fog which moved in and slowly covered the whole island. Adam's eyesight now became very limited because of the thick haze.

Now Adam was alone on the island with the dragon. He only remembered the dragon as a type of thought or perspective in his head. At first he was so upset with the dragon's perspective that he determined to stay as far as possible from him in his mind. This didn't seem to bother the dragon at all. In fact the dragon seemed to be in a state of intoxication, caught up with himself, his crown and what he now considered his island.

After many days had passed though, Adam became bored and lonely. The dragon saw this as an opportunity and began to speak to him again. Even though Adam only believed the dragon to be a type of mental perspective which formerly deceived and deeply wounded him, he seemed hopeful that the dragon might now be used to help him survive his isolation. I could see that to the dragon, the man was like a puppet whose only purpose was serving or entertaining him.

At first, the dragon's perspective seemed to be sincere and wise. But before long, the dragon had tricked him into wagering a portion of his freedom. Adam lost and bitterly left the dragon's perspective now with less freedom than he had come with. There he sat alone, isolated and embittered.

More time passed before Adam again began to suffer greatly with boredom and loneliness. It wasn't long before he came up with some new reason why the dragon's perspective might now be useful to him. As I watched this play out over time, I could see that this pattern repeated itself continuously. Every time Adam would allow the dragon a stage in his mind, the dragon always seemed to find a way to deceive him into surrendering another part of his freedom or portion of his life that meant something to him, and every time Adam would again isolate himself until boredom and loneliness prompted him to try again.

The Spirit said, "Boredom and loneliness are two great engines. They will either push forth creation or they will push forth destruction."

As time went by, the dragon's perspective truly left an imprint on Adam. It wasn't long before Adam had lost all purity and became a total subject of his environment. Soon, there was no choice that Adam made that wasn't decided out of fear, hate or loneliness. In misery the man and the dragon existed together year after year.

Chapter 13

The Dragon & His Bricks

TIME ON THE ISLAND BEGAN to fast forward rapidly and pass over decades and centuries of time. The descendants of Adam quickly multiplied upon the island. I saw them spread out and a great number of generations come and go. But then time slowed down again and I saw what looked like a busy and corrupt generation, a generation who had come to thrive under the rule of the dragon.

THE TOIL OF BUILDING THE DRAGON'S WALLS

The island was long and narrow. It was at least a few miles long and about 200 feet wide. On the farthest end of the island opposite the hill and the forest, the dragon had put the people to work building what seemed to be a maze of walls and rooms. There was no visible order to the layout.

The Spirit said, "His isolation has no order."

The dragon was jumping from one person's back to another; his legs seemed to conform perfectly to each person's neck as he perched upon them. Having them run back and forth across the island digging and cutting large stone bricks out of the ground, he drove them and worked them hard each day and night.

Even though the descendants of Adam could not see the dragon, they were very familiar with his voice. Yet, unlike Adam, they didn't even seek to make it separate from themselves. They accepted it without question as an intrinsic part of their own nature.

Each morning, the dragon made sure to visit each person and suggest to them a quota of work. He always made the quota small enough to seem possible, but always just big enough to be impossible to reach in one day. He also made many suggestions as to the harsh consequences that might await the descendants of Adam if they failed to reach the quota.

The dragon had shiny green and black scales all over his body. After he had visited each person, he would jump down onto the ground and begin to walk around in the midst of all the workers. As he walked around, the black scales would drop off him like seeds. Whenever one fell off him, another one would immediately grow back to replace it. Whenever one hit the ground, a large black rock brick would automatically spring up where the scale had landed. Everywhere he went these bricks would pop up around him like weeds.

The Spirit said, "Look closer at the bricks."

As I did, I noticed that each of the bricks had a different name etched into its side.

The Spirit said, "He usually starts to build with the same bricks."

The first brick I saw spring up was named PRIDE, the second FEAR, the next SPECULATION, the next ACCUSATION, then SELF-PRESERVATION.

The moment that a brick would spring up, all the people within about a fifty foot radius would turn their attention to it. The bricks seemed to have a magical pull to them. The people rarely questioned the origin of these black bricks. They didn't seem to recognize the bricks as something foreign or evil at all. Instead, some would treat them in reverence as if they were some type of idol or divine gift, and others claimed them as their own property as if the idea and project originated with themselves. Regardless of the motives, every time one of these black stones was created, the people nearby would use it as a boundary and foundation stone and begin to build a new wall, by placing their own stones upon it. Four or more of these stones would usually determine the parameters of their room.

If one combination or order of bricks didn't work with one set of people, the dragon would move on to another set of people. Then after a little time had passed, he would return to the former group and try another set or order of bricks. Some people groups took faster to the bricks then others. But no one seemed to recognize that the bricks came from the dragon.

The Spirit said, "He places the first few bricks then the people of isolation generally take over and place hundreds more. By the end, there is complete separation and division."

He continued, "This is the beginning of religious law."

These were the names of the bricks the people most often laid first upon the dragon's foundation stones: IDENTITY, SECURITY, RICHES, SELF-PRESERVATION, CONVENIENCE, COMFORT, SELF-INDULGENCE and COMPROMISE.

When the nearby people would gather around the dragon's stones, they would feel a warm sense of unity being together as one large group. After all, they saw each other as family, fellow workers and neighbors. But as they built their walls, a larger and larger barrier began to separate them. In the end, the result would be a total division between the group, half on one side and half on the other.

The more work put into a wall and the more a wall grew, the more the people would grow attached to it. They would take personal ownership over it. PROTECTOR was one of the most frequently used bricks. PROVIDER was also one of the most commonly used. They treated the wall as if it were their own father, their protector and provider. If they chose to keep building, which they almost always did, it slowly became the most important thing in their lives. It became the thing they loved the most, spent all their time on, and worshiped.

The Spirit said, "They have begun to love their bricks more than themselves."

Many of the highest bricks within the walls were named HATRED and FEAR. The higher the wall got the more they began to hate and fear the people on the other side. The people didn't realize it but every brick they laid was another brick that was used to isolate and box themselves in. They began to pride themselves on what they were not instead of what they were. They had false identities.

The Spirit said, "They know who they are not, but not who they are."

THE NATURE OF SEPARATION

Each enclosure usually had just enough room for them to feel free, but never at the expense of their control. The whole ordeal of separation required so much labor and pain to complete that once one segment of people had successfully boxed themselves in, they would often become obsessed with maintaining a maximum control over everything within their walls. Thus, the possibility of another separation would be limited if at all possible. They often boxed themselves in by pointing out the faults of all the other rooms and then comparing them to the strengths of their own room. At first the leaders themselves did not know their own motivation for maintaining such control and separation. They would say separation was in the best interest of the people. This was often true, but fear was present too. And in the long run, fear would always seem to gain more influence upon the motives of their hearts.

More often than not, over time, the men would become addicted to the control and power they had in the rooms that they had built. As time went on, every decision and every motivation became more and more rooted in the fear of losing control or power. They almost always justified their fear based motives by reasoning that it was necessary for the ultimate protection of the people. They had come to believe that their own existence, health, and prosperity were dependent upon their ability to secure and maintain control over their room.

The Spirit said, "They think the security of their room depends completely upon them. But actually it is them who depend completely upon it."

I questioned in my head, "Yes, but there is nothing wrong with wanting to steward or manage something unto the glory of God, is there?"

The Spirit answered, "God has called and created them to rule and steward, but not in this manner. He has called them to steward and rule over His creation and unto His glory. What they are doing is trying to rule and steward their own creation unto their own glory. If someone's ability to manage has become the primary source of their security and identity, then it has become an idol and an enemy of the faith."

After a moment, He continued, "This is the source of so much toil and strife in the world."

He continued again, "This is the way it is with the devil. He is the architect of islands. He gives you a platform and instructs you to build a wall around it. He then gives the illusion of you being ruler of this environment, but in reality, the whole structure is founded upon his lies. You might be able to maintain control by exerting yourself, but in the end it is you that is under the control of the devil.

Before this point, I was thinking that the dragon represented the devil, but I wasn't positive. Now, as the Holy Spirit referenced the devil, I became convinced. I turned to the book of Revelation and was surprised to find the scripture that says, "And he laid hold of the dragon, the serpent of old, who is the devil and Satan..." (Rev. 20:2) I also looked up the word "devil" in Greek and found that it is "Diabolos." I discovered that the word "diabolos" comes from "dia" which means "through," and "bolos" which means "to cast." The "devil" is literally a being who casts himself or something else "through" or "in between" two in order to separate them. This is exactly what the dragon was doing with his island and his bricks from the beginning.

The people on both sides of the wall would often try to box themselves in so they would not need to have any dealings with anyone else at all. I saw all kinds of families, friends, social classes, tribes and nations being divided in this way. Once the people had successfully boxed themselves in, they would rarely seek to leave their level. This gave them great security. The people rarely left their layer or room once secure. The dragon's goal was eventually to have every single individual be completely isolated with a wall built around him.

Every now and then a person would try to destroy a wall or a brick. The dragon took alert to this very quickly. He would stir up many of the people on both sides of the wall to take offense. An attack on the wall came to be seen as an attack on themselves. They would either quickly isolate the brick destroyer by building four walls around him, or they would throw him out all together in order to keep him from destroying all their hard work.

GOOD IDEAS

Then I realized that I kept seeing one type of stone that was a lot smaller than all the others. At first the stone was very hard to see, but once I saw it, I recognized that there were thousands of these stones placed everywhere all over the castle walls and floor. There was at least one of these small rocks for every large one.

The Spirit said, "The name of this stone is GOOD IDEA."

I saw that good ideas were being used as stabilizing rocks, being fit into all the small places. These were not truly "good" ideas for they were being built upon the foundation of lies and every one of these ideas was only placed to help fortify the divisive and destructive ideologies of man.

Each time someone would place one of these "good ideas," it would become almost impossible for him not to take the credit in his heart if this idea happened to be successful from a worldly perspective. The flip side of this of course was that it was also almost impossible not to take the blame in his heart if his good idea was not successful from a worldly perspective. Because of this, I saw that multitudes of people within each layer or room were either in condemnation and self pity or in pride and vain glory. There were also those under the influence of both at the same time, and they would flip flop between one and the other. It was odd to me that this flip flop could happen because they seemed like such opposite manifestations.

The Spirit said, "They are both manifestations of independence and pride."

These good ideas would cause so much trouble. Not only were they a cause of pride and condemnation, but since there was such a personal investment made into placing each one of these good ideas, those who placed them would take offense if anyone stood contrary to them. In the end, these "good ideas" almost always caused a greater wall to go up between people.

The Spirit said, "There is so much toil and vain glory because of this type of brick."

I questioned to myself, "But God has given us brains. Isn't it good to create, invent and make things?

The Spirit said, "Yes, I have given you a mind, but if you are not using it in unison with Me, what you create will be vain at best. Your mind was made to explore your union, not to invent division. I love when your imagination runs wild, but not when it runs wild in Hades."

After a moment He continued, "Like Adam and Eve. there are many who still come on a daily basis to eat from the tree of the knowledge of good and evil instead of from Me. Their ideas come from a false source. They must come to place their ideas upon the true Rock. Only then will their minds build in purity."

My eyes returned to the people building their stone structures. There were more and more fragments of people working tirelessly building their walls. Many walls were being built. Very few of the walls had doors but they soon began building stairways. Everyone wanted to be able to see and have a vantage point over all the others. Stairways would bring you to the top of your room so that you could have a vantage point over others. I saw many people perched upon the tops of their walls.

Building became such a part of their routine that they could do it without even thinking. Many of them would just zone out, with blank expressions on their faces as they worked. When one room would become secure, it was common for them to begin to try to find ways to build new walls within the larger one.

Some caught on and began to hate that they contributed to the walls. The dragon would throw some self-righteous bricks over and they quickly forgot their disgust for the walls and soon found themselves more isolated than ever. Some groups had successfully boxed in others; others had successfully boxed in themselves.

THE FORERUNNERS OF RELIGION

I saw the first story of these rooms quickly spread over the landscape. Before it got far, another group of people began to build a second story. This would enclose the people in the room below, like being in a big dark coffin with no way out forever. These walls stretched out farther and farther. The rooms and levels were being built up higher and higher.

There was a false sense of freedom held by those who built on the outermost layers of the dragon's twisted castle. These were the forerunners of religion. They expanded and built creatively, and reasoned that they were the pioneers of reformation. Their theology placed everyone under the power of sin instead of Christ. They imagined themselves the most free from the dragon's control; in comparison to everyone else. Yet they still built on the foundation of isolation and in conformity with the dragon's design. These were the ones responsible for contributing the most to the dragon's work. Because of this, the castle was quickly being built very high and wide. Running to and fro, building up walls through comparisons and differences, these outer builders were the ones most influenced by the dragon.

The Spirit said, "There are many of these in your generation, but they are quickly running out of room on their island."

In a unique way, the walls seemed able to trap in the mist and the haze from the nearby river, and it became increasingly difficult to see within the rooms. The people started bending down to read the bricks so they could make sure they were in the right, familiar place. They began to know their place in life by the bricks they walked on and near. These bricks became their navigation. Within a few generations, they had completely forgotten what the skies of open freedom looked like, and they had begun the evolution toward becoming a race of hunch backs.

THE FIRST TO FEAR

I looked at the dragon and for a moment, I saw in his eyes the same fear, anxiety and lust I had seen in the people he deceived. I was surprised to find that it stirred up feelings of pity for him. He was more a victim of lust and deceit than anyone. I saw he was once beautiful. While the people in the walls had the ability at times to see without the influence of fear, the dragon could not. He knew nothing of trust. He only knew security in himself, in his own power. He could not even understand union. He did not have the power to understand love or faith. He only had fear, speculation and unbelief. The only security and provision he could fathom was in his own ability to protect and provide for himself. He did not know who his father was. He could not see that he was also a creature created by a Creator. Because he assumed he was fatherless, he did not wait for his inheritance. Thus, he was driven to take one for himself. His relation to others was based only on what he could take from them. He found no pleasure or purpose in giving. The only way of survival in his mind was to take from those whom he envied. His jealousy and fear toward the children of God drove him to isolate, manipulate and control them lest they realize their dominion over him.

The Spirit said, "Even if he wanted to he could no longer understand or remember faith or love. He has condemned himself. His mind and will have become bewitched. He is now cursed without hope of repentance."

The Spirit continued, "You see, fear did not come first to Adam, but to the serpent."

My focus turned to the multitudes who were building their laws into the castle. Everything they built was founded upon the dragon's depravity. I became frustrated and sad. I wondered why they couldn't see and how come I could. I began to wonder where Jesus was.

At this point, I realized I had lost track of the dragon. I couldn't locate him anywhere.

The Spirit said, "He is in the floor and in the walls. He is present at the building of every new wall. And once a wall has begun, he moves on to lay the foundation stones of another."

My focus was upon the dragon's emerging building of chaos. My heart was breaking for the situation. It was almost too much to take in. I thought to myself, "The dragon represents the devil. The devil isolates, separates and divides, so this seems to imply that separation is bad. But there must be some types of separation that are good—separations that are from God and not from the devil."

The Spirit answered, "Yes, but the separation that comes by the hands of God is not petty. The only separation that God commands is the one that is from the island itself. It is a separation unto Union. There are some who have rejected the island of isolation and are looking for a different dwelling place, a heavenly one. These will be given power to leave the island. They will ascend the holy hill and enter the forest of God."

I thought of the scripture that says, "By faith Abraham, when he was called, obeyed by going out into a place which he should receive later for an inheritance; and he went out, not knowing where he went. By faith he sojourned in the land of promise, as in a strange country, dwelling in tents with Isaac and Jacob, fellow heirs with him of the same promise: For he was looking for a city which has foundations, whose architect and builder is God." -Hebrews 11:8-10

The Spirit said, "Let me show you the first to see."

Chapter 14

Abraham

THE FIRST TO SEE

INSTANTLY WE WERE BACK at a time when the dragon had just begun his building. As I watched the multitudes running to and fro, I saw one who was different. Day after day and night after night, he would not run too and fro with the rest. He would wake up and walk from the stone walls over to the far edge of the island, the edge closest to the forest hill where I stood. And even though he could not see through the mist, he just stood there staring up as if he knew there was a hill forest right on the other side. His great hope and belief filled in for his lack of sight and caused him to see. He just knew something more was there. It drew him.

Time seemed to speed up, and I saw many days go by. Every day he would come and stand there staring just as he had the day before. One day, time slowed down again and on this particular day, one of the trees up on the hill behind me bent way back with its top touching the ground. Then suddenly it released and sprung forth and as it did I saw a small shiny object shoot way up into the sky. As it came down, it landed right in front of this man. It looked like a seed that was in appearance like a shining diamond. The man picked up the seed in excitement and looked back up to see what else might come.

The Spirit's voice now spoke past me directly to him and He said, "Take this seed and eat it."

So the man took it, and he ate it. As soon as he had swallowed, the man took on the appearance of a great shining star like a diamond made of light. He now, with appearance as a shining diamond, was left with a unique ability to pull in and reflect light so that whenever someone from the island stood in front of him and looked through him just right they could catch a clear glimpse of the hill and its forest. The man stayed there motionless, day after day, year after year, with his focus locked strait ahead on the forest.

The Spirit said, "His name is Abraham."

I remembered Hebrews 11:8-10. It says, "By faith Abraham, when he was called, obeyed going out into a place which he should receive later for an inheritance; and he went out, not knowing where he went. By faith he sojourned in the land of promise, as in a strange country, dwelling in tents with Isaac and Jacob, the heirs with him of the same promise: For he was looking for a city which has foundations, whose architect and builder is God."

I realized that the Spirit was showing me something about Abraham, the father of our faith. I believe He was saying that Abraham's security and identity were not found in written laws and in walls built with human hands, but in God alone.

I remembered the passage in Galatians that speaks of Abraham. I turned there and read, "O foolish Galatians! Who has bewitched you? ...Does he who supplies the Spirit to you and works miracles among you do so by works of the law, or by hearing with faith— just as Abraham believed God, and it was counted to him as righteousness? Know then that it is those of faith who are the sons of Abraham. And the Scripture, foreseeing that God would justify the Gentiles by faith, preached the gospel beforehand to Abraham, saying, 'In you shall all the nations be blessed.' So then, those who are of faith are blessed along with Abraham, the man of faith." - Galatians 3:1-9

As I first read this I began thinking about how Abraham lived before the Law of Moses was given. That meant that his relationship with God was not based on the law. His righteousness and innocence before God was not based on religious rules, but simply on hearing and believing. This passage was saying that the New Covenant is a relationship not based on observing religious rules, but upon simply hearing and believing. It was saying that "He who supplies the Spirit to us and works miracles among us" does so, not because we fulfill some quota of the works of the law, but because we simply hear with faith. Our identity and operation should no longer be based on or motivated by our religious or political laws or *associations*, but based on our faith in Christ. "Maybe that's why some groups don't see many miracles, and others do." I thought to myself.

THE GOSPEL PREACHED TO ABRAHAM

The second thing that caught my attention was that the Gospel was preached to *Abraham*. I wondered how that was possible. How could the Gospel be preached to Abraham before Jesus ever died upon the cross? Wasn't the Gospel about Jesus on the cross? What was the gospel that was preached to Abraham?

The Spirit said, "The Gospel is that every nation would one day be blessed through his Seed."

I thought about how I myself, a "Gentile" had been blessed by Jesus and how I was a fulfillment of that promise.

The Spirit said, "You do not understand the blessing. Continue your reading."

I turned back to Galatians to pick up where I left off, "For all who rely on works of the law are under a curse; for it is written, 'Cursed be everyone who does not abide by all things written in the Book of the Law, and do them.' Now it is evident that no one is justified before God by the law, for 'The righteous shall live by faith.' But the law is not of faith, rather 'The one who does them shall live by them.' Christ redeemed us from the curse of the law by becoming a curse for us—for it is written, 'Cursed is everyone who is hangs on a tree'— so that in Christ Jesus the blessing of Abraham might come to the Gentiles, so that we might receive the promised Spirit through faith." - Galatians 3:10-14

The Spirit stopped me and said, "He became cursed so that He could gain access to the cursed. He became sin so that He could gain union with sinners."

"Hallelujah!" I thought. "That is amazing!" I pondered this for some time then eventually my attention turned back to what the Spirit had said, "You do not understand the blessing." In the last section of the passage, it read 'Cursed is everyone who hangs on a tree'—so that in Christ Jesus the blessing of Abraham might come to the Gentiles, so that we might receive the promised Spirit through faith." - Galatians 3:13-14

After reading the passage over again, I realized there was a link between the "blessing of Abraham" and "the promised Spirit." The promise God made to Abraham was that they would all be blessed. I realized the promise about the Gentiles being "blessed" did not happen during the incarnation of Christ. Christ did not go to the Gentiles, but to the lost sheep of Israel. Gentiles didn't really feel any blessing from Christ until Cornelius, a Gentile, was baptized in the Spirit many years later. I realized that the fulfillment of the promise God made to Abraham was that God's Spirit would be given to all Nations through his Seed! That's what the passage in Galatians was saying, "In Christ Jesus the blessing of Abraham might come to the Gentiles, so that we might receive the promise of the Spirit through faith." The Holy Spirit dwelling in all the Gentiles is the promise and goal of the good news! This meant that the aim of the Gospel had more to do with the immersion in the Holy Spirit than anything else!

The Spirit said, "Christ revealed who you are so that you would reveal who He is. This is His covenant—the exchanging of your identity for His. His incarnation is your identity. His Cross is your worth. His resurrection is your innocence. His Spirit is your resident."

After a pause He continued, "He made Him who knew no sin *to be* sin on your behalf, so that you might become the righteousness of God in Him. For as through Adam's disobedience the many were made sinners, even so through the obedience of Christ the many were made righteous." He said this, partially quoting 2 Corinthians 5:21 and Romans 5:19.

I paused to think about what He was saying. As I did, I looked at the star of Abraham and all the people who had gathered around him so they could see out of the castle of religion into the forests of freedom. They were prisoners on the island of isolation. I wanted to tell them of Christ. In fact, I wanted to tell everyone on the whole island about Christ. I wanted to lead them into their future, to help them escape. Yet, as I began thinking of ways I might do that, I hesitated. I suddenly didn't feel confident or competent enough to lead. How could I presume to lead them when I didn't even have a full picture? I started questioning if I ever really understood God's requirements for salvation in the first place. I knew what I believed theologically, but all this revelation made me question everything I ever thought I knew. I started seeking a clear answer. I asked, "What is required for people to be converted from being a "sinner" to being a "child of God?"

"You don't understand," the Spirit answered. "They are already the children of God, they just do not know their Father. They just do not recognize it is His image and His likeness that they were created in."

But as He said this I thought, "But not everyone is a child of God." I thought this, because I was remembering the passage that says, "But as many as received Him, to them He gave the right to become children of God, even to those who believe in His name." - John 1:12

A second passage came to mind, "By this the children of God and the children of the devil are obvious: anyone who does not practice righteousness is not of God, nor the one who does not love his brother." -1 John 3:10

"You are right." the Spirit said. "But I speak of mankind as a whole. Christ revealed the heart of the Father of all of creation. Of all of creation, man is the only one who is made in the Creator's image and likeness. For this reason, you are already His children. While this is true, it is also true there are many who have not been reconciled to their Creator and even others who oppose their Creator. These are not considered children because they do not accept Him as their Father. I desire all to be saved. I desire for them to know their origin. That they are dearly loved. That they have a Father who wants them if they will accept Him."

"Wow!" I thought. The way He was implying we should apply these truths was revolutionary to me. I felt like maybe I had been approaching people from the wrong angle all along. The message we preach should not just be about turning from sin, it should be about turning towards our origin in God. We did not originate in sin, but in Christ. We became sinners when we left our union with God and began governing ourselves. Before Adam was a sinner he was first a child of God. Christ came to reconcile man back to their original purpose and union with God. That is the message of reconciliation! The work of Christ is to return us to our original innocence and identity before sin ever entered our conscience. His work is to restore us and reconcile us to God's original idea of us. He came to convince us of our identity and worth so that we would not object to His presence and power within us.

THE OBJECT OF THE GOSPEL

I thought of what the Spirit had said, "His incarnation is your identity. His Cross is your worth. His resurrection is your innocence." These things Christ revealed about us so that we would believe His residence in us. This is the heart of the Gospel.

I started asking myself, "Why, after all these years, do I still consider myself a sinner when Christ calls me righteous? Why do I approach God as a foreigner when I was made in His image and likeness in the first place?

"False humility," I heard in my spirit.

I thought to myself, "Is that really the whole focus of the story of the Bible? Is the Bible really just the story about how God, through Christ, was reconciling all the people of the earth to Himself so that they would consider themselves worthy to receive His Spirit? Is that really the aim of the Gospel?" I started thinking of how, during the past decade of street ministry, I had so often made the Gospel about going to heaven when we die instead of about releasing God's Spirit in peoples lives.

The Spirit said, "The resurrection is only one of the benefits of your reconciliation."

He said this as if to correct the idea that heaven is *only* about this life. He wanted me to know that there was indeed a future resurrection and judgment, but the object of the Gospel from God's perspective was not heaven or hell, but His union with us.

As I thought through what was being said, I began feeling a big shift in my motivation and approach to the Gospel and toward people. Approaching someone as a sinner who is going to hell feels way different than approaching someone who is a child of God that has not yet been reconciled to their Father or empowered by His Spirit. Approaching people as condemned sinners, regardless whether it is true, fails to give them the dignity they deserve as those made in the image and likeness of God. In contrast, Jesus, during His incarnation seemed to approach everyone, especially "sinners and tax collectors," as if He was already married to them, as if they were already His treasured possessions.

The Spirit said, "Whatever you have done unto the least of these, you have done unto Me."

As He said this, I realized Jesus *did* indeed think of Himself as one with the criminals, prostitutes, tax collectors and sinners! Not that He was one with their sin, but that He approached them as if already convinced of His union with them. He didn't seem to come from a position of separation from the sinners, but of union with them already. Instead of thinking that their impurity could make Him dirty, He seemed to think that, if He could only get close to them, His purity would forever make them clean.

Then the Spirit said, "Religion is your critic, Christ is your advocate."

I thought of the passage, "What the law could not do, weak as it was through the flesh, God did: sending His own Son in the likeness of sinful flesh and as an offering for sin, He condemned sin in the flesh." - Romans 8:3

THE MESSAGE OF THE GOSPEL

After a moment, the Spirit asked me another question, "What is the message that Jesus taught His students to preach?"

I thought of many things, but I felt as though there was a scripture that the Holy Spirit wanted me to find. Thus, I began skimming through the Gospel of Matthew, asking Him to highlight it to me.

Matthew 4:17 was my first clue. It says, "From that time Jesus began to preach and say, 'Repent, for the kingdom of heaven is at hand.'

"Is that simple message the Gospel?" I questioned. I read on. In Matthew chapter ten I found where Jesus sends His twelve disciples out. He says, "And as you go, preach, saying, 'The kingdom of heaven is at hand.' Heal *the* sick, raise *the* dead, cleanse *the* lepers, cast out demons. Freely you received, freely give." - Matthew 10:7-8

"That's it?" I questioned. The message that Jesus taught His Disciples to preach was, "The Kingdom of God is at hand?" I thought about what that simple message was actually saying. It was saying, "God is close, stop thinking He is far." This is the simple message of the Gospel!

I thought of all the complicated preaching in the world today. Instead of making God close, so much of our Gospel preaching seems to make Him far–often very far, or only reachable for super holy people who are willing to go through any number of religious hoops. I had been approaching people from the wrong direction. I started to realize how big this subtle difference was.

I thought of the very last two verses in the Old Testament. They say, "Behold, I am going to send you Elijah the prophet before the coming of the great and terrible day of the LORD. He will restore the hearts of the fathers to their children and the hearts of the children to their fathers, so that I will not come and smite the land with a curse." –Malachi 4:5-6

As I consider what has been communicated about our father Abraham and the great white horse of faith, I can't help but think that God is saying that if we are going to move forward in our inheritance and understanding of His kingdom, we must allow our hearts to be reconciled with our fathers. Although I believe this ultimately speaks of reconciliation with our Father God, I believe God is saying that it has everything to do with receiving and learning from Abraham, the father of our faith.

I thought of Genesis 12:1-4 which says, "Now the LORD said to Abram, 'Go forth from your country, and from your relatives and from your father's house, to the land which I will show you; and I will make you a great nation, and I will bless you, and make your name great; and so you shall be a blessing; and I will bless those who bless you, and the one who curses you I will curse and in you all the families of the earth will be blessed.' So Abram went forth as the LORD had spoken to him..."

In many ways, this passage marks the beginning of Abraham's identity as the father of our faith. In it we see a complete trust and blind obedience to God. We also see an absolute security placed in God alone. We see the coming out from one identity, security, and covering and a complete reception of another identity, security, and covering which is in God alone. I believe the Spirit is saying that this is the model of faith we must return to as the children of Abraham if we are to fully experience the kingdom of God.

DESCENT FROM THE DRAGON'S RULE

As I watched the procession, I saw time fast forward again, only this time it wasn't as fast. Over the next couple years, a small but growing number of people began to disregard the dragon's command in order to come regularly to the diamond of Abraham and look up to the hill and its forest. Just like Adam, when these people saw the hill and the forest, it seemed to hold the answer to a deeply imbedded question. And even though they were not yet able to see or understand the magnitude of their dilemma, they knew something was wrong and that this forest somehow held the answer. When they came to look through the eye of Abraham, the mere sight of the forest caused them to behold two imaginations: there might be life beyond the island and the burdensome lifestyle of the island might be rooted in wickedness.

It wasn't long before the dragon noticed that some were missing. This didn't worry him too much because he knew there was no way off the island. However, he knew that if they were not kept busy, they might have more time to think for themselves. He thought he had better make an example of them before others caught on, so he put it in the people's minds to send out a search party to capture and punish those who were missing.

The Spirit said, "I give you the freedom to think and make choices for yourself. He fears and hates your freedom and your ability to make those choices. This is the nature of religion, and a major difference between his kingdom and Mine."

When the dragon had found those who had wandered off, he was greatly alarmed to find they could see out. He ordered that many of them be killed and that Abraham be buried.

His servants dug. Yet no matter how deep they buried him, there always remained a glow where the diamond had been buried. The dragon had all those who had seen it sealed into a tomb and increased the work load on the other side of the island so that no one would have any time or energy to consider anything else but their walls.

As the years passed, however, remnants of the legend of Abraham were whispered around the quarry. Before long, people began secretly searching for him. Upon locating him, they dug him out. And once again, light shown through him, enabling and enlightened the people to see the hilltop forest.

Chapter 15

Moses & Jesus

TIME SPED UP, AND I SAW many generations pass by before time slowed down again. This time the dragon had caught a large number of people who had seen the star of Abraham and the hill forest. But now, instead of sealing them into another tomb, he decided to convince everyone to establish a law forbidding anyone to go to the western side of the island where Abraham lay. They began building one great wall across the entire island. Their labor was increased drastically. He was trying to crush any dream of freedom. With many he was successful, for they began forsaking the idea of the forest. As a result, their memories were dimmed, and their hope was crushed.

The Spirit said, "This is the dragon's method for those who have once tasted and seen the glories of the age to come. He tries to starve them of their memory and crush their hope by increasing their labor and distancing them from the sight of it."

I heard the Spirit speaking to them, "I send you messengers to remind you. Listen to them, for My prophets can still see in times of blindness."

THE WALL OF MOSES

As He said this, I saw a man venture over to the place where Abraham lay, He looked very similar to Abraham. Like Abraham, this man also realized that he did not have to remain under the law of the dragon. Thus, he escaped and found a place to hide on the other side of the wall in the forbidden zone. There he spent his days like Abraham, looking up through the fog, believing there is more.

I was able to see this man's thoughts. He was able to differentiate between his own thoughts and the dragons. He questioned the dragon's power and authority to demand all of this labor. In fact, he supposed that he himself might have just as much authority and power as the dragon to create and establish law on this island.

He began to dig up the diamond of Abraham and kept doing so until it was completely unearthed. He took the dirt that was glowing from the star of Abraham and made a multitude of stone bricks out of it. He then took the bricks and made a large wall, stretching from the mote on one side of the island all the way to the mote on the other side of the island until he had successfully walled off where Abraham was to protect it from the walls of the dragon. This man's theory seemed to be true—indeed, he did have just as much authority as the dragon to establish law upon that island. He continued building until the wall stretched around on all sides, creating the feel of a big box with no top. With the bricks that this man made and placed, he created and established a different law which became a type of sanctuary and security upon the island of isolation. This place now seemed to be protected from the dragon and his influence.

Once he finished his wall, he went back to the dragon's castle and secretly started inviting people to come back with him. The laws he set up permitted him to do this and prevented the dragon from interfering directly. So before the dragon knew what to do, many had escaped and begun living within this protected courtyard.

The Spirit said, "This is Moses."

It was surprising to me that not everyone decided to come with Moses. For the ones who stayed, it seemed like even though their conditions were so harsh, they were at least consistent and therefore could be considered trustworthy and secure. When the dragon realized what was happening, he quickly came up with a new strategy. He began directing his people to build a large platform, stretching across the whole island from their former walls to the wall of Moses. When they reached the wall of Moses, the dragon commanded them to build up adjacent to it. I could see that the dragon thought that if he could build something similar and adjacent to the sanctuary of Moses, many would not be able to discern the difference between the two. Others perhaps might even be convinced to come back and work for him.

They built room upon room. When they had reached the top of the wall of Moses, they continued building until they had built a large walkway around the entire wall of Moses, which is where the dragon now stood. There they would look down upon Moses and the people within the sanctuary, and he would shout horrible things out to all of them. This made the people in Moses' courtyard very nervous, and they often complained to Moses about being down in his courtyard. Many of them were convinced to come back over to the dragon's side.

THE LAW IN PERSPECTIVE

I thought about how Moses' law was based on the island of isolation. Was the law of Moses good or bad? I had thought the law of Moses was good, but now that I saw that it was built on the island of isolation, I didn't know what to think. I began thinking of how the authors of the New Testament seemed to contrast Moses and the law against Christ and grace. If the New Testament authors treated the law of Moses and the grace of Christ as if they were in opposition to each other, that would mean that the law was bad. I decided to look up a few scriptures on the subject.

"For the law was given through Moses; grace and truth were realized through Jesus Christ." - John 1:17

"For through the law I died to the law, so that I might live to God. [20] I have been crucified with Christ; and it is no longer I who live, but Christ lives in me; and the *life* which I now live in the flesh I live by faith in the Son of God..." - Galatians 2:19-20

"You also were made to die to the law through the body of Christ, so that you might be joined to another, to Him who was raised from the dead, in order that we might bear fruit for God." - Romans 7:4

These passages seemed to suggest that we have already died to the law and no longer need to live by it. I said to myself, "Praise God we do not have to live by the law anymore."

The Spirit interrupted me, "I AM the Law. I AM that which I AM."

As He said this, it hit me hard. I instantly understood that Moses was only delivering the standards which He saw in God. God lives His law. The laws of heaven are merely some of the character traits of God. God revealed to Moses His personality and His environment. God keeps that law because God Himself is the personality of that law. He doesn't murder, doesn't commit adultery, doesn't steal, He keeps the sabbath, etc. These are all just extensions of His love.

It is not the law that is bad but the way we approach the law that can be bad. If we approach the law as if we need to keep the law to be like God, then we are living a lie already. Instead, we must approach the law as if we are already like God. I was discovering that the law is not as much a condition of His approval as it is a description of His nature.

"You must see the law from My perspective." The Spirit said.

As He said this, all of a sudden my perspective was changed. All along I had been looking at the courtyard of Moses' law as one standing on the island of isolation. Now the Spirit had shifted my position so that I was standing back up on the hill looking down at the castle from outside of it. I could now see a great difference in the two perspectives of the law.

Before, when I had looked at the law from the perspective of one who is isolated from God, I saw the law as the thing that stood between me and God. Going through the courtyard of the law was the only way to get to God, because God was on the other side of it. Now, standing with God, there was a sense of pre-existing union, as if I had existed there with Him long before the island or Moses' law ever became known. Together, we looked at the law of Moses in appreciation for the separation it had created, but at the same time, I also felt a bit worried. I saw the law as good, but it was not really helping the people on the island deal with the real problem of their isolation. A miracle still needed to happen to set them free.

I thought of the passage that says, "Why the law then? It was added because of transgressions... Is the law then contrary to the promises of God? May it never be! For if a law had been given which was able to impart life, then righteousness would indeed have been based on law. But the Scripture has shut up everyone under sin, so that the promise by faith in Jesus Christ might be given to those who believe... Therefore the Law has become our tutor *to lead us* to Christ, so that we may be justified by faith. But now that faith has come, we are no longer under a tutor. For you are all sons of God through faith in Christ Jesus." - Galatians 3:19-26

The law was given because of sin to show us we had left Him and needed to be reconciled with God, for we were no longer living like Him. Yet, the law was not given that we would start religions based on observing those laws but so that we would recognize we needed to be reconciled. Observing legal and religious systems of holiness cannot make us holy. Only accepting our origin and identity in Him can make us Holy. When we see the law from the dragon's castle, we see it as the thing between us and God. When we see it from God's perspective, the law becomes a sanctuary from sin because it is Him.

The Spirit said, "I AM my Law. I AM Love."

I stood amazed at Him. It is not that Jesus did away with the law, but that He perfectly embodied it. If we do not love, we do not have Him in us, because He is love, and the law is love.

If we are one with Him, we don't have to even think of the law because we will already be living it. The law is only a sign for those who think they are one with Him but are not living that way. Not operating in the law of love is evidence that something is wrong with your union with Christ.

THE ROCK CUT OUT WITHOUT HANDS

Again, time began to speed up, and it passed over hundreds of years. I could see the dragon's castle being built larger and larger with many different kinds and sizes of rooms. When time slowed down again, I saw that the entire island had been filled with layer upon layer of stone buildings. Some were still low and some had grown very high into the sky.

Then I saw a huge rock flying fast from over the forest hilltop behind me. It smashed right through the castle wall and landed in the courtyard directly on top of the star of Abraham. It was as if Abraham not only created a view out of the island, but also a view into the island. And now he was the target used to determine where this stone would be thrown!

The Spirit said, "Behold, the Stone cut out without hands."

The Stone was large and flat. Within seconds, it began to shake, as if about to erupt. Suddenly the sides started hatching, cracking and mechanically unfolding. I was taken to an ariel view and could see that the stone was unfolding and expanding like a river flowing in two directions.

In one direction, the stone was flowing deeper and deeper into the castle walls, smashing though every room that had been made on the island. It was as if the stone branches had the specific goal to punch through and create doorways and paths out of every room in the castle. In the opposite direction, I could see that the Stone had forded the misty mote and was growing in the direction of the mountain and the forest.

From above, it looked like a tree with giant roots that were filling the island below and endless branches that were filling the fields and mountains above. Stone paths now seemed to reach every place on the island and on the mountain.

As it finished expanding, it became quiet. Stillness filled the air. The stone had finished unfolding, reaching and filling every place it desired, both above and below. People from every room in the castle began to peek out. They could see again.

Where the Stone originally fell, on top of the star of Abraham, there was left a thin, rectangular, golden door. It began moving again. Abraham, after hundreds of years of relative stillness, had awakened and like a dead man rising out of his coffin, was now moving this great big stone that had landed on top of him. He picked up the stone and walked it over to the place where it had first smashed through the wall. There he set it down upright. It fit perfectly in the hole it had first made, and I could tell that Abraham was now setting it as a doorway. I felt the satisfaction that Abraham was feeling, having waited so long for a permanent way off the island of isolation and into the forest of life. I recognized this doorway now as the drawbridge I had seen earlier from where the white horse Faith was leading people out.

I began meditating on all that I had just seen and heard. I thought back to the fact that He had called the stone "the Stone cut out without hands." I thought this was an odd thing to say. What is a stone cut without hands? What is a stone cut *with* hands? As I asked myself this question, I immediately pictured little stone statues.

"An idol." The Spirit said.

I thought, "If a stone cut with hands is an idol, then a stone cut without hands must not be an idol." As I was thinking about this, I faintly remembered something like this from the book of Daniel. I turned there and found in Daniel chapter two Nebuchadnezzar had a dream and Daniel, interpreting it, said, "You continued looking until a stone was cut out without hands, and it struck the statue on its feet of iron and clay and crushed them. ...But the stone that struck the statue became a great mountain and filled the whole earth." (Dan. 2:34-35) Later on in his interpretation in reference to the stone cut without hands, Daniel says, "In the days of those kings, the God of heaven will set up a kingdom which will never be destroyed, and that kingdom will not be left for another people; it will crush and put an end to all these kingdoms, but it will itself endure forever.

I realized that the stone cut without human hands was in reference to idol worship. Stones cut with human hands are idols. The Stone cut without human hands must mean the uncreated One, that is the true God. The only One truly worthy of our worship, Jesus Christ, the stone the builders rejected.

Before the dust had even settled, a mass of people were already pressing at the gate. Someone found the lever and used it to open the gate for the first time. People from everywhere burst out of Hades and ran free. It was beautiful. It was just like I had first seen, except the white horse Faith was less visible. I saw flashes of him, but he wasn't as prominent. A number of passages came to mind.

"When he ascended on high he led a host of captives, and he gave gifts to men. In saying, 'He ascended,' what does it mean but that he had also descended into the lower regions, the earth? He who descended is the one who also ascended far above all the heavens, that he might fill all things." - Ephesians 4:8-10

"The path of life leads upward for the prudent, that he may turn away from Sheol beneath." - Proverbs 15:24

"Jesus said to him, 'I am the way, and the truth, and the life. No one comes to the Father except through me.'" - John 14:6

Time again sped up and passed over many generations. During this time, I saw the doorway open and close many times. Every time it opened I saw a different procession be released and begin their journey up the hill and into the forest. I realized our generation is by no means the only one that will ascend the holy hill and enter the kingdom of God. Indeed there have been many generations who have gone before us. Regardless of the age or generation, permission is granted for every generation who is willing to open the gate and follow the white horse of faith. All these have been permitted to leave the island of death and ascend the hill of life.

I remembered the verse where Jesus says, "Truly, truly, I say to you, I am the door of the sheep. All who came before me are thieves and robbers, but the sheep did not listen to them. I am the door. If anyone enters by me, he will be saved and will go in and out and find pasture. The thief comes only to steal and kill and destroy. I came that they may have life and have it abundantly." - John 10:7-10

And, "after this I looked, and, behold, a door opened in heaven: and the first voice which I heard was as it were of a trumpet talking with me; which said, 'Come up here, and I will show thee things which must be hereafter.'" Rev 4:1

Interlude

Given the last two chapters, Romans four and five seemed deeply relevant to me so I have included them here.

ROMANS 4

What then shall we say that Abraham, our forefather according to the flesh, has found? For if Abraham was justified by works, he has something to boast about, but not before God. For what does the Scripture say? "Abraham believed God, and it was credited to him as righteousness."

Now to the one who works, his wage is not credited as a favor, but as what is due. But to the one who does not work, but believes in Him who justifies the ungodly, his faith is credited as righteousness, just as David also speaks of the blessing on the man to whom God credits righteousness apart from works: "Blessed are those whose lawless deeds have been forgiven, and whose sins have been covered. "Blessed is the man whose sin the Lord will not take into account."

Is this blessing then on the circumcised, or on the uncircumcised also? For we say, "Faith was credited to Abraham as righteousness."

How then was it credited? While he was circumcised, or uncircumcised? Not while circumcised, but while uncircumcised; and he received the sign of circumcision, a seal of the righteousness of the faith which he had while uncircumcised, so that he might be the father of all who believe without being circumcised, that righteousness might be credited to them, and the father of circumcision to those who not only are of the circumcision, but who also follow in the steps of the faith of our father Abraham which he had while uncircumcised. For the promise to Abraham or to his descendants that he would be heir of the world was not through the Law, but through the righteousness of faith. For if those who are of the Law are heirs, faith is made void and the promise is nullified; for the Law brings about wrath, but where there is no law, there also is no violation.

For this reason it is by faith, in order that it may be in accordance with grace, so that the promise will be guaranteed to all the descendants, not only to those who are of the Law, but also to those who are of the faith of Abraham, who is the father of us all, (as it is written, "A father of many nations I have made you.") in the presence of Him whom he believed, even God, who gives life to the dead and calls into being that which does not exist.

In hope against hope he believed, so that he might become a father of many nations according to that which had been spoken, "So shall your descendants be." Without becoming weak in faith he contemplated his own body, now as good as dead since he was about a hundred years old, and the deadness of Sarah's womb; Yet, with respect to the promise of God, he did not waver in unbelief but grew strong in faith, giving glory to God, and being fully assured that what God had promised, He was able also to perform. Therefore it was also credited to him as righteousness.

Now not for his sake only was it written that it was credited to him, but for our sake also, to whom it will be credited, as those who believe in Him who raised Jesus our Lord from the dead, He who was delivered over because of our transgressions, and was raised because of our justification.

ROMANS 5

Therefore, having been justified by faith, we have peace with God through our Lord Jesus Christ, through whom also we have obtained our introduction by faith into this grace in which we stand; and we exult in hope of the glory of God.

And not only this, but we also exult in our tribulations, knowing that tribulation brings about perseverance; and perseverance, proven character; and proven character, hope; and hope does not disappoint, because the love of God has been poured out within our hearts through the Holy Spirit who was given to us.

For while we were still helpless, at the right time Christ died for the ungodly. For one will hardly die for a righteous man; though perhaps for the good man someone would dare even to die. But God demonstrates His own love toward us, in that while we were yet sinners, Christ died for us. Much more then, having now been justified by His blood, we shall be saved from the wrath of God through Him. For if while we were enemies we were reconciled to God through the death of His Son, much more, having been reconciled, we shall be saved by His life. And not only this, but we also exult in God through our Lord Jesus Christ, through whom we have now received the reconciliation.

Therefore, just as through one man [Adam] sin entered into the world, and death through sin, and so death spread to all men, because all sinned— for until the Law sin was in the world, but sin is not imputed when there is no law. Nevertheless death reigned from Adam until Moses, even over those who had not sinned in the likeness of the offense of Adam, who is a type of Him who was to come. But the free gift is not like the transgression. For if by the transgression of the one the many died, much more did the grace of God and the gift by the grace of the one Man, Jesus Christ, abound to the many. The gift is not like that which came through the one who sinned; for on the one hand the judgment arose from one transgression resulting in condemnation, but on the other hand the free gift arose from many transgressions resulting in justification. For if by the transgression of the one, death reigned through the one, much more those who receive the abundance of grace and of the gift of righteousness will reign in life through the One, Jesus Christ.

So then as through one transgression there resulted condemnation to all men, even so through one act of righteousness there resulted justification of life to all men. For as through the one man's disobedience the many were made sinners, even so through the obedience of the One the many will be made righteous.

The Law came in so that the transgression would increase; but where sin increased, grace abounded all the more, so that, as sin reigned in death, even so grace would reign through righteousness to eternal life through Jesus Christ our Lord. (NASB version)

Chapter 16

The Woman Being

AGAIN, TIME SPED UP, and I found myself passing over the time which I had previously seen. I again saw the gate opening for our generation and that it was triggered by a shift in the worship of the saints, who instead of balloons learned to carry banners. I watched as many chose to follow the white horse of faith onto the path leading into the Kingdom of God. I watched as they came out and experienced all the trials I had seen them go through earlier. I saw the darkness come and the three lamp holders step forward to give light to the procession, and then again I saw them fall. I saw the lamps being given to each person, and with one accord I saw them begin to march forward. Then, I again saw Death moving through and striking the people in the procession with his scepter.

I now stood back at the exact time and place I had left off when the Spirit had said, "I must show you your beginning." I could see Death, wreaking havoc on the procession with his scepter and the whole front end of the procession now looked totally disorganized.

As I watched, I saw the entire procession vanish and then reappear two times. I felt the Holy Spirit was saying this is a picture of our current generation. The procession must look different each time with different trials and tests for every generation.

I remembered the merchandise of Death was compromise. As Death moved through the front portion of the procession and hit person after person with his scepter, they became self centered. The compromise that resulted came in a number of weird manifestations. Some people just stood still. Others shut their eyes out of fear or doubt and either stood there still or fell on the ground with closed eyes. Still others when hit, turned around and started heading back to the castle because it was familiar and they knew they had already conquered it. I noticed many of the ones going back were ministers and pastors who had now come into the habit of receding in the faith.

THE STRATEGY OF DEATH

The strategy of Death was to attack the front of the procession closest to the white horse so a bottleneck would be created that would block the progress of the rest of the procession. This is exactly what was now happening.

At the head of the procession, Death now dismounted and sent his covered wagon ahead of him. One could see that his horses had been trained for war as they took aim and began charging forcefully at the most crowded sections of the procession in order to mow the people down. The whole sight was very intimidating, especially if you were in a cluster of people. As a result, there was a strong temptation to try to spread out so you were not part of a group the horses would target. As the people scattered, Death was able once again to infiltrate and use his scepter on them. It was a total mess. The procession was breaking apart.

The only encouraging thing I could find was that even through all the madness, there was still a strong number of unified people, with their attention on the white horse of faith. I could see that the black horses, who carried the wagon of compromise, were repulsed by these people. They saw them as a stone wall that could not be mowed down. While most of them could not really move forward through all the chaos, at least they were not retreating or losing their focus.

A CLOWNING MOVEMENT

Then I saw something unexpected. It was as if a bomb went off in the middle of the united group. It was not a bomb from outside, but a bomb from within. Even though they kept their focus on the white horse, they were also aware of the disarray of the procession as a whole, and most of them couldn't help but want to gather the scattered ones back. But instead of calling everyone back in gentleness, they were accusing and threatening them. This started with a few, but like a chain reaction it spread to almost everyone in the once united group. This is the bomb I saw go off, which scattered them as well. The result of all the accusation was a critical spirit that now took its aim at everyone, even those truly focused on the white horse.

I then saw another group of people emerge who looked completely different. These people started jumping around and acting really goofy and silly. The sight of them in the midst of the battle scene offered a shocking contrast. I hated to admit it but it was a bit comical. There were fearful, discouraged people who were battling Death on one hand, then a bunch of somber critics on the other, and now these fearless, goofy, clowning, people going bonkers all over the battle field with big smiles on their faces. It was bizarre. I didn't think it would be appropriate to laugh, but I wanted to.

I could see that these clowns had once been part of the united group and I could tell by the look in their eyes that many of them had the purest intentions. The jubilation, goofiness and freedom of these funny people was attractive to me and I could see that much of it came from a place true purity and steadfast rejection of the religious systems of the castle. However, many of them blamed the critics within the procession for the dysfunction and disunity instead of Death. The irony was that while their clowning was a direct offense against the critics of the religious system, much of the clowning itself had become merely a different form of criticism.

I realized that now, I too had become critical towards all of them. I realized that we were stuck. In this environment, everyone would eventually lose their focus and become critical of others, or at best overly self-critical. No one could see the white horse anymore.

I was devastated. How could we find any hope. The procession was stopped. Some people stood with eyes closed, some had been mowed down by Death's compromise, others had turned back, others were standing there criticizing everyone and still others were clowning the critics. The entire front portion of the procession was defeated. Death had succeeded. No one was looking at the horse. No one was focused on where they were going. Everyone was acting independently.

"I hate Death." I said in utter frustration.

THE WOMAN

But then I saw from the back of the procession, a beautiful and radiant woman came and stood right in front of Death. She was different then all the others. She was totally pure. She was bold and unafraid, unaffected by Death and his scepter. Dignity and glory radiated around her. She was the most beautiful thing I had ever seen. She was so beautiful that her beauty alone exuded strength. Her beauty caused a fear to well up within all who saw her that she might be spoiled from association. I felt shame even to look on her. I felt dirty. I felt untouchable. She wasn't very tall but she had a very long white train that flowed behind her as she moved.

She was talking to the Spirit continuously and the Spirit was talking to her. She walked up to death and spoke in a soft stern voice, "You have been commanded to leave and to return to your island. You have no more business out here on the path of life."

Immediately his power was stricken from him and he was hurled back onto his island.

As this was going on, I noticed that the Holy Spirit was changing. It was as if I could see His eyes. Before this, I had known Him only as a type of presence, a type of breath. Now He was beginning to take on a form. Even though I could not totally see Him in detail, I could see that He now had the silhouette of a man. As His shape filled in more and more, one could see that He was absolutely FIXATED on this woman. In love, the Spirit now became almost bashful, very touchable. He now took on the full form of a man.

He whispered as He fixated on her, "For her, I became a man; for her I took on human flesh."

The Spirit whispered with joy in His voice as His eyes followed every move of this woman. In admiration and respect He said to me, "Her name is My Church—My Bride. Her train is Love!"

I looked at the long train that flowed behind her as she walked. I could see that all who went before the bride had become counterfeits and she held all the true host of heaven in her train. This was the true procession. She was not only sure of what she was leaving, but positive of where she was going. With great grace, she led the procession on its final steps through a passage in the trees and into the hilltop forest.

The Spirit said, "Without love, no one can see My kingdom. Many, many have fallen and forsaken My love for the sake of their castle."

As He said this, I saw 1 John 1 in my mind. I felt like I should read the first epistle of John. As I did, there were a number of verses the really spoke to me.

1 John 3:14 says, "We know that we have passed out of death into life because we love the brethren. He who does not love abides in death."

1 John 2:9-11 says, "The one who says he is in the Light and yet hates his brother is in the darkness until now. The one who loves his brother abides in the Light and there is no cause for stumbling in him. But the one who hates his brother is in the darkness and walks in the darkness, and does not know where he is going because the darkness has blinded his eyes."

1 John 3:10 says, "By this the children of God and the children of the devil are obvious: anyone who does not practice righteousness is not of God, nor the one who does not love his brother."

1 John 4:8. says, "The one who does not love does not know God, for God is love."

I also remembered what Jesus said in Matthew 24:12 concerning the last days, "Because lawlessness is increased, the love of many will grow cold."

The Spirit said, "To everyone the Father loves, He gives light and life. Light is the knowledge of God and life is knowing God."

As He said this, I thought of John 17:3 in which Jesus says, "This is eternal life, that they may know You, the only true God, and Jesus Christ whom You have sent."

The Spirit continued, "The law of love has two children. Their names are Life and Light. These were the two trees of the garden. All true love will give light and life to her recipients. Because of His love, He grants us light and life."

I thought, "But I thought we weren't supposed to eat of the tree of the knowledge of good and evil–the tree of light. I thought eating from that tree is bad."

The Spirit said, "Everything in the garden was good–including the tree of the knowledge of good and evil. It was not eating it that was bad, it was disobedience and disunity that was bad. Your Father's will has always been to enlighten you. But enlightenment does not come from disobedience. It comes from union. If you come to understand good and evil independent of your union, then the light through which you see is truly darkness."

I thought of the passage where Jesus says, "But if your eye is bad, your whole body will be full of darkness. If then the light that is in you is darkness, how great is the darkness! - Matthew 6:23

THE LANDSCAPE OF LIGHT

It was now still and peaceful. The sun was beginning to rise in the east. The Spirit seemed to stand next to me as I looked out at the scenery. I had seen so much from this vantage point. I had an urge to join the procession as the front portion of the procession began to enter the forest at the top of the hill, but as soon as I began to walk over, I got a strong sense that the Spirit had at least one more thing that He wanted to show me from this place. After a moment of stillness, I looked off to the north and south a great distance. It was as if the Spirit was comparing the size of the castle to the size of the rest of the world. It was as one might imagine. The castle was on a parcel of land which was only a few miles long and about 500 feet wide. The rest of the world was about the size of the rest of the world—huge in comparison to the land of the castle.

I asked, "Is there anyone else born anywhere?"

It was such a vast place and struck me odd that all the people would just be concentrated into this one little island.

He said, "Yes. You were born right here. This is the place I first conceived of you. You were born here long before you were born there." He paused for a moment, allowing me to think on what He had said. "And No." He said, "Where else would they come from? The only way out of Adams island is by the courtyard and its procession."

This was a bit confusing to m. What He was communicating was beyond the limits of my understanding, yet I gathered He was talking about the two births that Jesus talked about with Nicodemus.

"[Nicodemus] came to Jesus by night and said to Him, 'Rabbi, we know that You have come from God *as* a teacher; for no one can do these signs that You do unless God is with him.' Jesus answered and said to him, 'Truly, truly, I say to you, unless one is born again he cannot see the kingdom of God.' Nicodemus said to Him, 'How can a man be born when he is old? He cannot enter a second time into his mother's womb and be born, can he?' Jesus answered, 'Truly, truly, I say to you, unless one is born of water and the Spirit he cannot enter into the kingdom of God. That which is born of the flesh is flesh, and that which is born of the Spirit is spirit. Do not be amazed that I said to you, 'You must be born again.' The wind blows where it wishes and you hear the sound of it, but do not know where it comes from and where it is going; so is everyone who is born of the Spirit.'" - John 3:2-8

After reading this I started thinking that the Spirit was saying that in the flesh we are born as children of Adam on the island of isolation, and in the Spirit we are also born as those who always existed in Christ. The question He seemed to be presenting was the same question He had raised so many times already on this journey, "Which one do you associate more with, the body of Adam or the body of Christ?"

At this time, everything seemed to slow down. I began noticing how beautiful creation is. As I looked at the scenery, I began feeling the vastness of time and space–the vastness of God's imagination. I can't find words to describe the infinite things I was feeling at that moment. My mind could not take in what my spirit was seeing. Everything was so truly amazing.

He spoke again, "There is so much to explore once freed from Death. Death is such a small and populated place. Heaven has much more to explore, there are many mansions hidden in the deep forests and mountain tops. They are for you to find and explore. You will find your own mansion here. Yet you are not exploring material, but light. Light is truth; Light is the revealing of truth."

He continued, "There are many nearsighted. All those in the castle are nearsighted. They can only see and believe what is right in front of them. Their eyes fail even to see the sky."

I remembered that within the castle walls, most of the levels which people existed upon were top levels with an open roof. Yet with hunchbacks, few, if any, ever looked up.

He continued, "They are able to see the sky. But they are not willing to see it. They often only want to verify that their own walls are secure."

Again, He continued, "What you are seeing is not material, but light. It's revelation. You are seeing in the spirit. The only light given to those in the castle is that which they are willing to see and believe. What you are seeing is not land, but light—this whole vision. The Father has birthed all men into a world of light, a world of sight—much more a world of light than a world of earth. While Adam began with open sight, he dimmed that sight by isolating himself. It was that man Abraham who was farsighted. Because of his belief, light was able to pierce through and a doorway of light was established upon the island of the isolation of man. When the rock cut without hands did His work, He gained access to all of Hades. From that time forward, whenever someone has come to His path, there is enough light to see outside of the island and up to the heavenly forest."

He continued, "Many men are only willing to see the light of death— that is, the light of natural law. All things of the natural are of death. The only light and revelation given to the natural man in the castle is the revelation of death. This is the way of all life if isolated from its Author. Remember, you can only go as far as you can see and hear."

After a pause He continued again, "The castle's name is Law—all mans law. The only revelation that has been given to the natural man is the law. The law is death. Yet, the law of the Spirit of life in Christ has set you free from the law of sin and death. So now that the Spirit has come, man can see life. But he cannot see life unless he is willing to look outside of his own walls—his own natural walls. Only then can he come to know the overruling and transcending laws of love, life and light."

As He was speaking of the natural law, I understood it to mean that which does not take into account the supernatural (like God). The Spirit seemed to be pointing out that the mere existence of life, light and love are contradictions of anything that would deny the supernatural. I concluded then that the "natural man" that the Spirit was naming is the one who denies all things supernatural. According to the Holy Spirit, this would ultimately have to include love, light and life, because the laws and sources of such things are supernatural, transcending the dead, natural law.

I thought about how the Spirit had said that the law of love and her two children, life and light, are laws that transcend all others. The trees themselves grow strait up in contradiction to the law of gravity—even the life that is within a tree has the power to contradict the laws of death and gravity. Life seems to exist and contradict death if and when it pleases. Similarly, light has the power to contradict darkness— light always dictates the borders of darkness, but darkness never has the power to dictate the borders of light. The sacrifices of love also must have the power to contradict the powers of fear no matter where you are in time and space.

The Spirit spoke up again, "All revelation given to man in this age is only the revelation between life and death. Most are only willing to see death. The procession is filled with those who were willing to see life. They are on the journey now to see if they truly want to enter it. All the light you have seen so far of God's revelation is the tiny path between death and life. You have yet to explore the rest of My imagination, the rest of My light. It is filled with deep truths, and vast truths, and new colors and new sounds. There is so much more ability to perceive light once released from the walls and island of Death."

Then I asked the Spirit, "Why can't we all just be born in the Kingdom of light to begin with?"

"You do not understand what you ask." He said. "In the beginning, I created the light. The world is a world of light and you are all born into the light. This is your true origin—not sin, not darkness. You all belong to Me. All is My domain. The fact that you can see anything at all is testimony to the fact that you are all in My kingdom. The rain falls on the just and unjust and so does the light. There is no partiality. All the earth and all it contains is already Mine. You are born as My own. And while it is My desire for everyone to know Me, it is not yet so. So now you ask why are not all born with the full revelation of who, and where, and why they truly are?

He continued, "I have allowed it for your own good. I have allowed it because I want you to decide who you are. I want you to choose how much like Me you really are. Light enables identity, and identity demands distinction. Who are you?"

"What about all the evil? How is all this for our own good?" I thought to myself.

He answered, "Light was first given as a grid from which My image and likeness could experience Me. Only those who see the difference between light and darkness can choose between light and darkness. My love gives you freedom to decide who you are. The trials you face in your earthly life, although I despise many of them, are allowed so they can reveal you. They only last a short time and then all is made manifest. You tend to question My justice in light of the presence of evil. Yet you forget that evil is temporary. Righteousness and justice are not denied; although they might seem delayed. All who live righteously do receive their reward. The judgment that you all speak of in the future is being lived out every day by your free will. It is good for you to decide who you are. It is good for you to distinguish between Me and you so that you can decide that you would never want to be separated from Me."

He continued, "To experience Me is to experience love, and to experience love is to experience true freedom. The very fact that people are permitted to reject Me is a testament to My love for them. My love does not demand reciprocation. Love is the only government under which true freedom can be found. Without the freedom to reject your Maker, you would never have freedom to love like your Maker. How do I reproduce My offspring? I give them freedom and power. This is how I am. How could My children be anything less? Without freedom you would never know who you are. Many people have yet to make a decision out of freedom. Many have only made decisions within the castle, and subject to the castle. They only know fear of rejection, fear of failure and the fear of man. Until they come to know My love and grace, they will never be able to make a true decision. They can only make it from their broken heart and broken flesh."

He concluded, "If My image and likeness has come to experience separation, it is only in order that they fully appreciate union."

He had said so much. I paused for a while to try to soak it all in. I thought back to how He said, "I want you to choose how much like Me you really are." I thought back to Genesis 1 and how it says that we are made in His image and His likeness. Then reading on, I realized this was the very thing the serpent caused Eve to question. He said to her, "For God knows that in the day you eat from it your eyes will be opened, and you will be like God, knowing good and evil." She was already like God, but here, the serpents words got her to begin approaching God as a foreigner, as one in exile. The serpent's subtle trickery got her to believe that she was not like her own Father God already.

"The origin of all sin." the Spirit said. "The illusion of separation and distance."

I began thinking, "So is the castle just a facade? Is it an illusion that the devil has created to get us to think there is distance between us and God when there really is none?

"There is," said the Spirit.

I thought of the passage that says, "Although you were formerly alienated and hostile in mind, *engaged* in evil deeds, yet He has now reconciled you in His fleshly body through death, in order to present you before Him holy and blameless and beyond reproach." - Colossians 1:21-22

I understood Him to say that the distance is real, but that the distance is rooted in our minds—its in the way we think. I realized the only way the devil can be successful in separating us is if he can trick us into believing we are far from God or foreign to God.

The Spirit said, "The measure of light you perceive is the measure of life you'll receive. Without having light, you could never know yourself. The measure of light is the measure of identity."

He continued in a more stern voice, "However, do not lust after light. For the deeper the light you see, the weightier the choices you will be responsible for making. See," He said, "Light is useful. Revelation forces you to decide and define who you are. To some people, Light is an enemy who comes only to condemn. To others, Light is a friend, who comes only to enlighten. To the one, Light reveals them as lustful, fearful creatures. To the other, Light reveals them as righteous, loving creatures."

He continued, "As it is with light, so it is with freedom. The greater the freedom you experience, the greater you will come to know yourself and," He paused for a moment, "in this case, your need for Me. For all those whom I love I also give the freedom to decide what and whom they will love. Love causes you all to decide who you truly are, without the sense of intimidation from Me. I will not control anyone. Limited revelation causes you to make decisions from your heart. This is what I want. It forces you to make decisions of your own. "

He continued, "I gave you light so that I might show you your need for union with Me. I want you to decide that you really are more like Me than anything else and therefore that you really are worthy to inherit the kingdom."

"You are my instrument of sufferings. I created you that I might be shown perfect through sufferings, perfect in love."

Again He continued, "Many are born; heaven does have children. It is just a different birth—not of location, but revelation. As the Word and the Spirit are declared, light and power is given and a bridge of life is lowered. An open door is presented, those born from above will see and enter the kingdom—because they are looking. I planted a seed and it spread from Abraham. This is my harvest."

Colossians 1:9-14 says, "For this reason, since the day we heard about you, we have not stopped praying for you and asking God to fill you with the knowledge of his will through all spiritual wisdom and understanding. And we pray this in order that you may live a life worthy of the Lord and may please him in every way: bearing fruit in every good work, growing in the knowledge of God, being strengthened with all power according to his glorious might so that you may have great endurance and patience, and joyfully giving thanks to the Father, who has qualified you to share in the inheritance of the saints in the kingdom of light. For he has rescued us from the dominion of darkness and brought us into the kingdom of the Son he loves, in whom we have redemption, the forgiveness of sins."

Chapter 17

The Forest
& the Kingdom of Heaven

AS THE PROCESSION BEGAN TO ENTER the forest the Spirit said, "Come up here and I will show you things you have not yet seen."

I turned and walked toward the hill forest. As I got closer, the air seemed to change. The sight was like nothing I had ever seen or felt before. There was this aura like a rainbow of light that glowed above the forest at the top of the hill. The air was more brilliant, pure, and colorful than anything I had experienced before. The air over the forest was so crisp and clean that you were able to see farther—much farther than I had ever seen before. You could see as far or as detailed as you wanted. I noticed the dew on clouds that were many miles away and in the next moment, I looked upon the microscopic intricacy and order that made up a single pine needle. There was so much detail it felt like I could stand there for a thousand years and never see all there was to see.

The Spirit told me, "The name of the hill forest is "Life." The name of the river, "Lust." Both Life and Lust have many faces."

As He was speaking, great winds were striking the castle and shaking it. The winds were blowing in a direction towards the hill forest. The wind desired to pull all things in. The wind was so strong that it seemed like it would have been easy even for the island's stones and its water to have been taken in by it if they were willing. But just like the people within, they were not. The thought of being "taken" by anything was against their very nature and contrary to anything they had come to know.

I remembered the verse in John 16:8 that says that when the Spirit comes, "He will convict the world regarding sin and righteousness and judgment." And then the words of Stephen in Acts 7:51, "You men who are stiff-necked and uncircumcised of heart and ears are always resisting the Holy Spirit; you are doing just as your fathers did."

The Spirit said, "Lust is like its river. Lust is like its walls."

He was now calling the river of "Lust" the river of "Death."

He continued, "Look at how the river flows, it shows a face of Death. The path of Death is like its water, the path of least resistance. It is always searching for the quickest and easiest way down. Death's river has been given power only to move the things that stand in the way of its downward progress. Its source is lust and its destiny is death. Its water is one of the most destructive elements allowed on earth."

The Spirit was comparing the water to the people in the castle. At this point, I thought of the river of God in Ezekiel. I also thought of the rivers of living water that Jesus said would flow out of our innermost being. I thought to myself that He couldn't be saying that all water is destructive.

The Spirit answered, "Water can bring life under the right government, but it is a destroyer when its energy is not being channeled in the right direction."

He continued, "Now look at the trees. There you will see one of the faces of life. Observe how tall they are, yet they grow so slowly that it looks as if they were not growing at all. It takes great strength and patience to grow as tall as they have. The path of life is often the path of greatest resistance. They grow straight upward against all ease, in spite of all elemental improbability, in spite of the gravity of this world. The law of Life defies and transcends the law of nature itself. All Life has been given the power to contradict the laws of Death in order to grow upward, against the flow of Death and decay. Life has been given power to remove all things that stand in the way of its upward path. The tree starts from one source and branches out to many giving life. Every season bears a new height and a new width, and a new set of leaves."

THE TREES AND THE CASTLE

The focus now seemed to change from the river mote to the walls of the stone castle. As the Spirit's voice shook the castle, He continued, "My voice sounds upon the castle as a hurricane. I desire to break them out—to set them free, but the people inside the castle are only hoping that their castle will be able to withstand the force of My breath. They fortify their walls against Me! They protect themselves from My Kingdom. The castle is an abomination which must be destroyed. Yet the Lord tarries in hope that more will escape its destruction."

He continued, "Behold the rock walls and their likeness to those within them. The rocks themselves are rigid. When a strong force rises against them, they'll rather break than bend. Sometimes as you have seen, there are slight shifts and cracks, yet these are more a result of the will of man than Me. The trees in contrast are so eager to bend and to move and to mold to the shape of my breath. They are not uprooted, but they do yield. They always move when I breathe on them. The rocks are rigid and unforgiving. Such is the nature of Death. Stiff, still, heavy to move, unchanged by My will and My breath, yet easily manipulated by the hands of willing men. Life is like the trees—always adjusting to Me, always able to change, move and grow, always feeling its way up. Although living within the walls offers you a form of security against the winds, the trees offer you a form of security against the letter. As they are rooted in God, they are moving in My Spirit."

As I heard this I thought of the passage that says, "...[God] has made us sufficient to be ministers of a new covenant, not of the letter but of the Spirit. For the letter kills, but the Spirit gives life." - 2 Corinthians 3:6

THE HILLTOP

After some time, I remembered that the procession had begun to enter the forest and for some reason I thought that if I didn't join the procession quickly, I might not be able to access the forest. So I joined the procession near its end. We were led through an opening on the side of the hill forest; it was as nothing I had ever experienced before. It was as if heaven itself was actually touching the earth in this place and that the earth was responding as a lover. The forest seemed to be a pine and redwood forest—like the forests in the mountains of northern California. They were all bent down in reverence. It struck me again how much brilliance was there. There were no words for it. All the people seemed to find places to stand, kneel, sit or lay on the trees. It looked like a giant stadium that held a million people. There were many others that had been waiting for us there. The horse called Faith was there, standing in the middle and watching us all fill in.

We stood there for a long time waiting for all the assembly to find their places. After what seemed like many hours of discovering different fascinations, I began longing to share this experience with those who were also there with me. By one's self, you almost thought you could be hallucinating or dreaming, but experiencing something so supernatural with another person made it so much more believable and receivable. I looked around trying to make eye contact in order to share just a mutual look of thanksgiving toward God, but as I looked, I noticed that many who were there were not noticing the glory that shone upon them. They were there, but absent. They were sons and daughters of the Most High—they had gone through so much to enter the kingdom only to disgrace it. I felt a deep sadness and shame and I became angry.

I thought of doing something, saying something to them, I was on the verge of yelling, but then I heard the Spirit's assurance, "Shhhhhhhh, be still. I will change this."

Hearing His voice set me back into the ecstasy of His glory and His presence. I realized that in taking my focus off Him and placing it on others, I was missing the point as much as any of those upon whom I focused. I repented and fixed my thoughts on Jesus.

As I did, the Spirit said, "You will come to know a greater glory that is yet to be revealed in all of you. When He is revealed, no one will be distracted. Where sin abounds, grace abounds all the more—Christ in you, the hope of glory."

As He said this, I was shaken to the core. "Christ in me is the hope of glory?" I questioned.

"Glory has a hope!" I said to myself.

"Yes." The Spirit responded, "Glory's hope is that you would understand in the incarnation of Christ was His becoming one with you and with all flesh. He became the Son of Man so that you might know that you are the Sons of God."

It seemed like the Spirit was not just talking to me but to many of the people who were there, because everyone was starting to look more in awe of their surroundings and in expectation of Christ.

After enjoying a long time of just the mere glory of this place, the last of the procession made it in. The stone giant who was called the Word of God was at the very end of the procession and as he entered, His body sealed the entrance way. Every single seat looked like it was now filled. At this time, a great hush fell upon the people. Something within every person was drawing us deeper and deeper in an immediate expectation of Christ. It was as if all of a sudden, everyone knew that all things were about to change forever.

"The fullness of the Gentiles has come." I heard being whispered among many of the older people who had been waiting in this place from times of former processions.

Then a Voice came from the horse and uttered words that were pure and Spirit. The language felt familiar, but I had never really heard it with my ears before. The words and sounds were beautiful without blemish. Pure power came from them. I felt them pounding and passing through my soul and my spirit. Although I could not understand mentally what was being said, I still knew what was being said. It seemed to be a different type and level of communication that was more perfect and exact than I had ever experienced before. I could tell that He was not speaking to the assembly of men, but to the trees which were behind us. As He spoke they moved as by wind. It was not violent, but as if they chose to move simultaneously and in agreement with His words.

The interpretation of what the voice was saying to the trees was, "Bring forth the contribution which you have been storing up for your kind."

It struck me that it did not feel awkward when He commanded the offering to be taken as often as it is when requests for contributions are made. It felt right to ask for the contribution. I could tell the trees didn't feel awkward at all. This contribution was something that they had anticipated for a long time, and it gave them great release to finally accomplish it.

The Spirit said, "This is how it is for all of us who have been waiting so long to give."

As He said this I thought of all the times I had so little to give because I had never stored up in anticipation to give. Because of this, my giving, especially if it involved sacrifice, was rarely a joyful thing. I got a sense that the Spirit was saying that this is the way it is with things the Spirit has been longing to release. It brings all who love the will of the Spirit joy and great relief to finally release their contribution; to finally see the glory come to fruition, even if it means great sacrifice for either party.

The Spirit said, "Some have heard My call, but instead of saving up for their contribution, they dread it and begin to spend all they can on themselves before they have to come to it. To the Lord and His saints it is because of the joy that is set before them that they store up things to give and love."

THE MAN OF LIGHT

After the Voice had given this command to the trees, in front of the horse, I saw the ground began to crack open like an egg. A small shoot slowly begin to rise up and grow. After a good length of time, it grew up into a tree about 10 feet tall. It was not like a normal tree; it was all thick and deformed. After it had stopped growing, with what looked like an enormous effort, with reverence and great strength, it bowed down before the horse. At that moment, with the multitude of mankind looking on, a great light shone from upon the horse. As the light shone, you could discern that the light had a face. The light was in the form of a man. I realized that the man had been on the horse from the very beginning, but no one's eyes were granted sight of Him until now.

The Spirit's voice trumpeted, "All hail King Jesus!"

It was Jesus Himself upon the horse! Upon the first moment of realization, I was overwhelmed at the idea that my eyes would finally get to look on Him who died for me—my Messiah, my Savior. But as I tried to look at Him, His light gave off such a great amount of heat that it felt like it would burn away everything it saw. Every person present flinched, recoiled and hid his face. It was part out of reverence, but mostly it was just out of mere survival. It felt like our flesh would be burned off if we allowed His glory to shine upon it.

The Spirit said, "As with Adam, so it is with all mankind. It is not that the Lord hides Himself from you, but that you hide yourselves from Him."

I wondered why the light was so hot.

The Spirit said, "With all light there is heat."

He continued, "Light begets heat just as knowledge begets movement. The purer the light, the stronger the heat. The purer the knowledge, the stronger the movement. There is a light so bright and strong that naked and natural eyes fail to look upon it. For this reason, no flesh except that which has died can withstand the light.

I remembered in John 1:9 where it says, "There was the true Light which, coming into the world, enlightens every man." And John 8:12 where it says, "I am the Light of the world; he who follows Me will not walk in the darkness, but will have the Light of life." And in 1 John 3:19 where it says, "This is the judgment, that the Light has come into the world, and men loved the darkness rather than the Light, for their deeds were evil."

I also remembered a few of the scriptures that speak of Gods fire.

Deuteronomy 4:24 says, "For the LORD your God is a consuming fire, a jealous God."

"Who among us can live with the consuming fire? Who among us can live with continual burning? He who walks righteously and speaks with sincerity, He who rejects unjust gain and shakes his hands so that they hold no bribe; He who stops his ears from hearing about bloodshed and shuts his eyes from looking upon evil;" -Isaiah 33:14-15

I began thinking to myself that the whole time it was Jesus who had been riding on the horse, but even the church was not beholding His radiance until they came to the proper place of faith, hope, love and expectation.

"Yes." the Spirit said, "You can only see what you believe."

I was reminded that in the spirit world, light and revelation make up reality and that if I hadn't formerly recognized Christ upon the horse, it was not because something physical stood in my way, but because something spiritual stood in my way. But now His light shone, and as it did, I caught glimpses of my surroundings. Again I was struck by the fact that it was so much brighter, crisper, infinitely brighter and more vibrant than anything I could have imagined before. I thought of the polarizing contrast between the visibility of air at the forest compared to the visibility of the air at the castle.

Within the castle, on most of its levels you could barely see the bricks in front of you. That's why they all had such hump backs within the castle. So long as they subjected themselves to the rules and laws that governed their birth floor, they were limited in seeing anything beyond it. I realized that while I myself was in the castle, I could scarcely discern that there was a darkness and fog that didn't belong there—I had just accepted and learned to live with the darkness and fog, never knowing that it could be any different. I recognized that in the past, I had even allowed myself to adhere to the idea that I shouldn't expect to see clearly. But now as more light was allowed in and I was brought to a place where I could see into Christ and His kingdom without limit or blur, I realized how dim and how paralyzing it was to live within the borders of the kingdom of darkness. Seeing within the realm of Him who rides the white horse, all of us, with infinite sight, could view everything as crisp and as clear and as far and as near as we desired."

Chapter 18

The Light of Life

THE NATURE OF LIGHT

JESUS, WHO I WAS SEEING as this Man of Light, dismounted the white horse and began walking toward the twisted tree in the midst of the assembly.

The Spirit said, "From this tree the fruit was taken. Upon this tree the Lord replaces. This is the tree of the knowledge of good and evil."

I was shocked. I would have expected this tree to be in Hades. I didn't know what to think.

He continued in a soft, reverent tone, "This is the time that changes all others."

It did not seem like what we were now seeing was in chronological order, but that we were seeing things more in the order of spiritual significance. What I was now seeing I understood to represent the center of all time and history according to the records of this realm.

As Jesus came near the tree, a brilliant flash of heat and energy went out and the tree suddenly burst into flames. As this happened, the assembly immediately fell to the ground half in wonder and half in fear.

The Spirit said, "It is He who comes to baptize in Spirit and in Fire."

No one dared move an inch.

Then the worst thing happened. The Man of Light lay down upon the tree that was on fire and He began burning. His skin became black and hard, and His light became concealed. All was utterly dark once again. You could not see anything at all anymore. I was devastated! How could someone so beautiful and powerful, One whom we needed so badly do this? What would it mean for us? Would we ever see again? No answer came.

The Spirit whispered, "He is the fullness of the knowledge of good and evil. He returned what was taken by Adam."

It was obvious that I was not the only one devastated at His actions. All you could hear was loud whaling and bitter weeping coming from everywhere in the forest.

It seemed like a number of days went by in complete darkness. No one cared about time though. No one moved, except to weep.

After a long time, the Spirit said, "The grave cannot keep Him."

I looked up and began to see a tiny glimmer of light. I could not tell if my eyes were adjusting to the dark or if it was actual light. But then I saw the ground crack and a ray of light burst out from the charred body of Jesus— then another, and still another! His outer flesh was charred and burnt, but it was beginning to crack and a new light was shining forth, bringing that limitless clarity that we had once experienced. As this new light began to illuminate and shine forth again, we could all see what looked like an unending flow of blood that came out of Him. His blood first began to flow down toward the root of the tree.

Then as His blood dripped down, every drip seemed to create a deeper and deeper hole in the ground where it landed. After a long time, these drips had created what looked like a deep well. There was a pure water that began to surface and then it gently began to flow out from under the tree and go into the forest toward the greater mountains. This was a different kind of river from the one around the castle. It flowed up hill in the opposite direction.

The Spirit said, "The name of God's river is Grace."

All of a sudden it hit me that the burning tree that the Spirit named the tree of the knowledge of good and evil was the cross of Christ! It represented the contribution that all the trees had been waiting to make since time began towards the redemption of the world and of man. I felt indebted to the trees and so thankful to them for making this awful contribution. I could see they felt a bit to blame for producing the tree in the first place.

I also realized at this time that the fire itself was the presence, the light, and the heat of the cross of Jesus and the presence of God. This is the place where no darkness can exist. This is the fire that Christ would come to baptize us into. I had always wondered what was meant by the baptism in fire. Some have said that it is judgment of God and we want nothing to do with it, and others say it is the Spirit. While these might be true, I have now come to believe that it is so much more. The fire of God is the presence of God, the presence of God is the judgment of God, and the judgment of God is the Cross of Christ. For those who surrender and allow the presence and fire of the cross of Christ to consume their life, they will gain eternal life.

It was hard to take it all in, but at the same time I started wondering, if the tree of knowledge of good and evil was here, where was the tree of life?

Upon this thought I was instantly taken by the Spirit way up above the forest to where I could see all of the island of Hades and the forest of the kingdom from an ariel view. Looking down from this height, one could see that the rock cut without human hands had made a beautiful design in the ground as it had unfolded. It looked like a giant two-dimensional tree had been etched into the earth with its grey roots on one end filling the entire island of isolation and its green branches on the opposite end filling the forested mountains of the Kingdom of God. The trunk of the tree, which was the pathway of the procession, was the link between the grey roots at the bottom and the green branches on top.

As I watched, the grey roots began taking on a dark red color. It was the blood of Christ flowing down from the tree of fire. The blood carved deep grooves throughout the surfaces of the stone walkways. The blood had now made its way all the way down from the forest to the castle.

The Spirit said, "Roots red with the water and blood of Christ."

The roots, which reached every room in Hades, were now being filled in with the water and blood of Christ.

From ariel view, I could see the roots stretching to every room in Hades as well as the branches stretching to every tree in mountains of heaven. Its source and its destination were both perfect. The stone pathway now acted as a channel for the water mixed with blood to flow into everything.

The Spirit said, "The river of heaven. It's source is the cross of Christ."

I thought of the passage that says, "He who descended is Himself also He who ascended far above all the heavens, so that He might fill all things." - Ephesians 4:10

It was odd to me that the tree had anything to do with Hades. Was this supposed to be the river of heaven which flowed from the throne of God? This picture made it seem like the roots (which is the life source of the tree) were rooted in Hades. Its epicenter was at the gate of the castle and not in the forest. I thought, "How is the tree of Christ rooted in Hades?"

"Do you still not understand?" The Spirit said, "Faith reaches higher. But love reaches lower. And hope continues to reach no matter how long."

He continued, "Your Faith reaches toward heaven, and in a way that is what true faith does, but it is as if you think you were not yet here. And there is no love but from heaven. I enjoy when you reach toward Me, but there comes a point when you arrive in the One you reached for, and finding My full embrace, you realize that I am always reaching back down, and have been all along. So like Me, you turn also to reach back down."

He continued again, "You have said that faith is rooted in the future, but I tell you that true faith is also rooted in the past. True faith remembers the work of Christ and lives according to it today. The only way you can see His future is through the lens of what He did in the past. Faith leads you on the path of what has already been given to you in Him. Faith points every obstacle back to Christ's triumph over it. Faith rests itself in Christ."

After a pause, He continued, "True faith will always mature into the sacrifices of Love. Faith is love's inspiration. Love is faith's manifestation. If you believe, you will love."

THE GARMENTS OF LIFE

After some time the Spirit took me back into the forest on top of the hill. I was in awe of everything. I thought about the tree of life and how big it was. It filled all of Hades and all of Heaven.

At this point the Spirit said, "This is the Tree of Life," as I felt Him tug on my sleeve.

I looked down and saw the clothes that grew up around me at the star of Abraham.

"What?" I questioned. This violated a lot of ideas that I had about the tree of life. "How could my clothing be the tree of life?" I questioned. At this moment I had a flash back to the times we had planted the seeds and the fruit on the sides of the hills. I realized that all of the trees of the forest of Heaven had at one time been planted by one of us. The seed was His word and the hills our hearts. A tree had grown for every act of obedience to His Word. The whole forest, all the greenery, was the fruit of our garments. The fruit of our works. Heaven was made of our works.

"Heaven is made of His works in you." The Spirit said.

"Wait," I responded, "I thought the Tree of Life was blocked off from humanity right now."

"Jesus is the Life." I heard in my spirit.

I didn't really know what to think.

I had another question. "But this looks like there are millions of trees of life. I thought there was only one Tree of Life."

It was silent, but I thought about the passage in Revelation that talks about the tree of life.

"Then the angel showed me the river of the water of life, bright as crystal, flowing from the throne of God and of the Lamb through the middle of the street of the city; also, on either side of the river, the tree of life with its twelve kinds of fruit, yielding its fruit each month. The leaves of the tree were for the healing of the nations." - Revelation 22:1-2

My hair stood on end. The tree of life is on both sides of the river of God, just like I had seen from above and its not one tree but a species of tree that has twelve fruits. Apparently, I was seeing something similar to what John was seeing, that the tree of life was everywhere! I began to wonder if this was a literal tree that is on earth that we just don't know about yet.

"Wait," I thought again, "What about those merchants who traded for the fruits from our garments back at the river of lust? Does that mean they will live forever?

"Yes." I heard in reply, "In a way they will. But the tree of life grows according to the soil it is sown in. It will produce fruitful life if it is planted in fruitful soil, but it will produce barren life if it is planted in barren soil. If they are not connected to the vine, they will not produce good fruit."

I remembered the passage, "I am the vine, you are the branches; he who abides in Me and I in him, he bears much fruit, for apart from Me you can do nothing." - John 15:5

THE LAST COMMAND

At this time the tree of fire gently set Jesus down on his feet. As it did this, all the remaining char broke off Him, and pure, brilliant light filled the whole mountain top. It was so bright and so hot that no one could remain sitting or standing. Everyone laid face down wherever they could find a place.

Many hours, days, weeks and months seemed to go by. No one was concerned with time in this place, and even if they were, there was no place that anyone would have considered worthy of their time more than here. It was perfect un-wasted time.

Then I felt the Spirit suggesting that I look up again. I didn't really feel like it, but I decided I had to at least try. I turned my head to the side and quickly opened my eyes for just a moment. I didn't try to look at Jesus, but only at the people who were laid out next to me. I could see that everyone was still laying face down. It struck me again how much clarity of sight and light there was.

At this moment Jesus spoke again in His heavenly tongue. It was very clear. He was giving orders to all the people to stand. I didn't realize this before, but now I could see that everyone had unknowingly sat in a pattern which looked like a military formation. I could now see that indeed this is what it was for there were captains and generals and soldiers. There was a direct purpose in the placements of all who were gathered.

Jesus then began speaking in a multitude of tongues with layers of tongues upon layers. It seemed like Jesus was giving specific orders to every individual in the place. Those at the far end of the stadium of trees began filing out toward the entrance. Even though He was still too bright and brilliant to look upon, I could tell that Jesus had remounted his horse and had moved to a place near the entrance where we had first come in. He was now watching and waiting for all of us.

In mechanical order, the people were all lining up and passing under the tree of the knowledge of good and evil and entering into the river of Jesus. It was a baptism of fire and water—a baptism into the cross of Christ. At the base of the tree it was extremely hot with red and white coals but there was also water—a well on which it now seemed to stand.

As we went through this baptism, our whole bodies including our eyes seemed to be burned and remade to be able to exist within the light of this place. As I realized that my eyes had been renewed, it instantly struck me that now I might possess the power to look on Jesus without hindrance. As I swung around to see if this was true, I realized that everyone else was doing the same and had had the same realization.

As my eyes found Jesus, it was shocking. I did not expect to see Him in the way that I saw Him. He was a dark sooted and bloodied Jesus who sat upon His white horse. He was focused and confident, eyes burning with fire, staring at all of us. His robe which was radiant like ours was also covered in blood and soot.

The multitude of people were now gathered and standing in military formation as if ready to charge at Christ's command. The mere sight of Him was frightening. He was serious, and He pointed toward the castle. Then with finger still stretched out, He swung over slowly, eyes piercing, and pointed at everyone including me.

As His finger came and fixed on me, He said, "I want you!"

It was like He was simultaneously saying this to many, if not all the people. I knew what He meant when He said this. He didn't just want me to stay there and lay on the ground. He wanted me to get up and accept the authority I had to be in that place. He didn't want us to carry around shame anymore. He wanted us to know that we were completely qualified to carry His power and His word.

The Spirit said, "The serpent makes you into slaves, the Savior reveals you as sons."

I thought, "But we are called to be slaves of God throughout the new testament."

He said, "No. I desire for you to first be sons, then some, if they mature, will graduate into slavery. For my kingdom is free and therefore its sons and daughters are free. Just as a king might have many sons, but only one will inherit the role of king, thus becoming a slave to it, so also God calls many His sons, but only a few are chosen to be apostles and slaves to the Gospel."

I thought of the passage that says, "So the last will be first, and the first last. For many are called, but few chosen." - Matthew 20:16

I realized that Paul always called himself a bondservant, but to others he emphasized that they were sons and daughters. Paul had matured as a son so he forsook his freedom and yielded his body as a slave to spread the

Gospel. I thought about how so many of our churches first teach servanthood, then sometimes sonship, instead of the freedom of sonship, then perhaps servanthood.

My focus returned to Christ. He was manifesting Himself now both as Warrior and Commander. He was looking for volunteers who were unashamed of the Gospel, those who would be willing to forsake their freedom as sons in order to serve the Church and the Gospel as slaves. It almost felt like a test. We were already included in His salvation. We were already in His family, but would we be willing to serve in His army as well? He was asking if we would be unashamed to give our lives for the sake of His gospel.

He ordered the volunteers to assemble at the mouth of the forest where everyone could see the Island of Hades. Then, pointing at the island, He said, "The age of Hades is at an end. The abomination that causes desolation is about to descend, for it has lost almost all of those who are ascending. Yet, there are still a few sons and daughters in its walls."

As He said this, everyone knew He was asking us to go back one more time to save the rest of those who were destined to ascend. At that point, all the people who were present stepped forward.

Then Jesus spoke to His horse and although I could not hear Him clearly, I knew that He had said something along the same lines of what He had earlier spoken to the trees. "Bring forth your contribution." As He said this it was as if He were speaking to the entire horse species. The great white horse let out a loud and joyful sound and an army of white horses immediately emerged from out of the forest as if they had been waiting for this moment all their lives. The horses walked up and found a partner. There was one horse for each person in the kingdom.

At this point, the Stone Giant (The Word of God) said, "I tell you the truth, this generation will certainly not pass away until all these things have been accomplished. Heaven and earth will pass away, but my words will never pass away."

Jesus said, "Let us now perfect this age of grace."

As He said this, He (as the Light of Life) and the Stone Man (as the Word of God) were revealed as One. They had never been separate. They had only been different manifestations of the same person! The newly revealed Jesus now appeared as a mix of the two. He was terrible and beautiful.

I remembered the scripture, "I saw heaven standing open and there before me was a white horse, whose rider is called Faithful and True. With justice He judges and makes war. His eyes are like blazing fire, and on his head are many crowns. He has a name written on him that no one knows but he himself. He is dressed in a robe dipped in blood, and his name is the Word of God. The armies of heaven were following him, riding on white horses and dressed in fine linen, white and clean." - Revelation 19:11-14

Then a thunderous command came from His mouth, "Go!"

THIS MARKS THE END OF WHAT WAS REVEALED TO ME IN ACCORDANCE WITH THIS VISION.

FOR OTHER BOOKS & RESOURCES

BY JACOB REEVE, GO TO:

www.thegoldenlampstand.com

8056438R00116

Made in the USA
San Bernardino, CA
28 January 2014